ADVANCE PRAISE FOR *THE QUEER EVANGELIST*

"Living on the street, using drugs, abandoned by the adults in her life, all while identifying as 'queer' in a hostile world—any one of these things could have unravelled many of us. Cheri hauled herself up and not only survived but thrived. I love that this strong, brilliant, competent woman has told her story so honestly."
— KATHLEEN WYNNE, former premier of Ontario, from the Foreword

"Cheri DiNovo has lived an incredible journey. She's been a street kid, a Sixties rebel, a doctor in ministry, a Reverend, and one of the most influential socialist parliamentarians in Canadian history. Tireless revolt against the injustice of the status quo runs through her life like an unbroken thread. She tells her story rapidly and with good humour. She never loses you, and you can seldom put the book down. This is essential reading not just for those interested in queer and socialist histories but for anyone who wants a riveting, humane tale of a woman who decided that the oppressed should make their own history."
— ARASH AZIZI, author of *The Shadow Commander: Soleimani, the US, and Iran's Global Ambitions*

"A deeply powerful memoir from one of Canada's most courageous feminist activists. An instructive tale on the perseverance of unapologetic activism from a woman who has dedicated her life to creating justice through activism, spirituality, and politics. Canadian activists can all benefit from DiNovo's frank, sharp, and generous retelling of a spirit born to create social change."
— SANDY HUDSON, Co-Founder, Black Lives Matter-Canada

"I've long admired Cheri DiNovo as an intrepid, passionate, inspiring activist, but I had no idea she had such an intriguing life story. From her early days growing up in an eccentric, matriarchal family, to her teen years dabbling in street life, drugs, and politics, to her transformation into an effective rebel against the establishment, *The Queer Evangelist* is a riveting tale. And through it all, her insight and her quest to make the world a better place comes shining through."
— LINDA MCQUAIG, journalist & author

"What a life! From street kid to church minister to politician and back, Cheri DiNovo fights for social justice and equality all the while practicing compassion and honesty even in electoral politics. An astonishingly honest life story told by an extraordinary person who breaks boundaries wherever she is. A brutally honest picture of the life of a socialist politician who is making change within the system, combined with an eye-opening vision of progressive queer feminist Christianity, *The Queer Evangelist* will challenge your assumptions, whatever they are."
— JUDY REBICK, author of *Heroes in My Head*

THE QUEER EVANGELIST

THE QUEER EVANGELIST

A SOCIALIST CLERGY'S
RADICALLY HONEST TALE

CHERI DiNOVO

WILFRID LAURIER
UNIVERSITY PRESS

Inspiring Lives.

Wilfrid Laurier University Press acknowledges the support of the Canada Council for the Arts for our publishing program. We acknowledge the financial support of the Government of Canada through the Canada Book Fund for our publishing activities. This work was supported by the Research Support Fund.

Library and Archives Canada Cataloguing in Publication

Title: The queer evangelist : a socialist clergy's radically honest table / Cheri DiNovo.

Names: DiNovo, Cheri, 1950- author.

Identifiers: Canadiana (print) 2021009012X | Canadiana (ebook) 20210090456 | ISBN 9781771124898 (hardcover) | ISBN 9781771124904 (EPUB) | ISBN 9781771124911 (PDF)

Subjects: LCSH: DiNovo, Cheri, 1950- | LCSH: Legislators—Ontario—Biography. | LCSH: Political activists—Ontario—Biography. | LCSH: Clergy—Ontario— Biography. | LCSH: Sexual minorities—Civil rights—Ontario. | LCSH: Sexual minorities—Legal status, laws, etc.—Ontario. | CSH: Ontario—Politics and government—2003- | LCGFT: Autobiographies.

Classification: LCC HQ73.73.C2 D56 2021 | DDC 323.3/26092—dc23

Cover design by Heng Wee Tan.
Interior design by Michel Vrana.

© 2021 Wilfrid Laurier University Press
Waterloo, Ontario, Canada
www.wlupress.wlu.ca

This book is printed on FSC ® certified paper. It contains recycled materials and other controlled sources, is processed chlorine free, and is manufactured using biogas energy.

Printed in Canada

LAND ACKNOWLEDGEMENT

This land was a sacred space long before my grandparents came. To our First Nations whose understanding of the Creator and Creature inspires and educates. We commit to standing with you as you continue your search for justice.

DEDICATION

This book is dedicated to all my sisters, some mentioned here and many unmentioned, who've birthed me, mentored me, loved me, and educated me. Your history-changing herstory is breathtaking. Thank you.

TABLE OF CONTENTS

FOREWORD

Queen's Park is the better for Cheri DiNovo having been a member of the Legislature. And Ontario is a better, stronger society for her participation in political life.

I didn't know Cheri DiNovo at all until she arrived at Queen's Park, but from the outset I felt I knew something about her motivation because she was a United Church Minister and because I have been a member of the United Church all my life. We never talked about it early on but I felt that she was in politics for all the right reasons. It turns out that she and I were baptised in the same church, Richmond Hill United: I, when I was a toddler with my two sisters in the 1950s, she, as an adult, decades later, consciously choosing the Church to live out her activism.

Cheri was elected in a by-election in September 2006, just a few days before Premier Dalton McGuinty appointed me to his Cabinet as Minister of Education. I had not been deeply engaged in the by-election but I had been in the riding of Parkdale–High Park a number of times to campaign for our Liberal candidate because this was the riding that had been vacated by Gerard Kennedy, a friend and Minister for whom I had worked as Parliamentary Assistant. We wanted to hold his riding. But Cheri was a strong, articulate candidate who won the day.

Cheri's telling of the story of that campaign is chilling for me to read as it lays bare the worst of the political process—a personal smear campaign. It was my party that would have supported, if not initiated, that campaign. But more than that, as an openly lesbian candidate, I have lived through my own personal smear campaigns. They are exhausting. They damage families as they damage democracy.

Cheri survived that campaign as she did so many extraordinary challenges in her life. She lays out, in detail and with honesty, the chaos of her early life. Just as I was thinking that it was amazing that she could hold herself together, she wrote, "It's incredible that I'm alive at all." Living on the street, using drugs, abandoned by the adults in her life, all while identifying as "queer" in a hostile world—any one of these things could have unravelled many of us. Cheri hauled herself up and not only survived but thrived.

I love that this strong, brilliant, competent woman has told her story so honestly.

When Cheri would stand in the Legislature to ask me a question, whether as Cabinet Minister or as Premier, I knew it would be a tough question grounded in truth. She talks in the book about the policy of inclusionary zoning that, if implemented properly, could lead to the construction of thousands of affordable housing units. I was supportive and wanted to see us implement the policy, which we eventually did, but when she started asking the question there was no appetite in our Government to do so. That tension made her questions really hard to answer—the best kind of Opposition questions.

Cheri is very tough on the political process but she judges all parties equally. She is an equal opportunity critic of political machinations. Understandably, our opinions diverge on a number of the incidents she describes, and only on one issue will I correct the record: Glenn Thibeault was not offered a Cabinet post before he decided to run for us in Sudbury. I know that is the case because only I could have offered him one and I did not. But it is so instructive for all of us, elected officials and not, to hear her unvarnished perspective.

Cheri's story is so much more than her political story. The Queer Evangelist has fought her whole life to improve the lot of women, of the queer folk who populated and continue to populate her life. Her understanding of "queer" is, she says, pre-linguistic. It is who she has always been.

I knew her as a fighter for LGBTQ2S rights. I saw her use the legislative process to bring people from different parties together for trans rights, for the rights of queer parents, for the naming and commemoration of historical travesties. I participated in her radio show with women from other parties and praised her when she introduced young women to the parliamentary process through her Girls Government initiative.

Cheri tells her story, a woman's story. By doing so, she helps to flesh out the narrow, straight, male story that colours all of our lives and institutions. I am grateful to her and honoured to call her a friend.

Kathleen Wynne
December 2020
Alliston, Ontario

PROLOGUE
BERNICE AND THE BIBLICAL TWO-STEP

At Emmanuel Howard Park United Church (now Roncesvalles United) in the late 1990s and early 2000s we had built an evening service around a free dinner. It had, over time, attracted a congregation very different from the morning service. The evening service comprised folk who were street-involved. Many were queer. Most had addiction and/or mental health issues. Of course, the morning service folk had mental health and addiction issues too. The difference, at its core, was money.

I have a story to tell. Not only did the protagonist, Bernice, give me permission to tell it, but she demanded that I tell it. So here it is, Bernice.

Bernice was a member of the evening service. She was about seventy years old at the time of this story and had been living "rough" for a great many of those years. Bernice pushed around her belongings in a shopping cart until eventually she landed in subsidized housing. Undoubtedly, like many others, her background was one of trauma and abuse. Without much access to shower facilities, Bernice carried with her the odour of the street. Without access to nutritious food, she'd grown large on starch and empty calories. Every Sunday night at dinner Bernice sat alone off in one corner of our Fellowship Room. One night I thought I'd try to change that.

I approached with some small talk and then said, "Bernice, why don't you come and join us at our table? There's no need to sit here all on your own." I was trying to be nice.

Bernice looked up from her plate of canned corn and smothered meat, clearly irked that I'd interrupted her meal, and with a heavy air of condescension replied, "Do you see those young men at your table? If I go over and sit with them, I'll drive them wild with lust!"

I've retold her story many times and it's always accompanied with laughter. Bernice laughed later too when I told it. She laughed because I was so clueless. The laugh was really on me. I'll tell you why at the end of this book.

Bernice was that woman. The woman we think we know but don't. How little do we know each other? In that instant I understood my own patriarchal indoctrination, low self-esteem and boring reality. I'd internalized the message that old doesn't equate with "sexy," that attractive means what advertisers tell you is attractive, and forgotten that there are more deliciously hidden desires in everyone that remain imperceptible. Anyone who's done psychedelics will know, like some physicists do, that reality is fluid. Our common sense is common but sometimes doesn't make much sense. Bernice is one of the saints who populate my experience.

There were others in that evening service too: George, who danced through every service, a kind of a back-and-forth hip-shaking number whether music was on or not. Danny, difficult to look at because crack and booze had distorted his features, yet he dropped a fistful of change into the collection plate every Sunday. His offerings were a far greater percentage of his income than the most generous morning service donor. Jim, who knew the lyrics of every song, read philosophy, knew scripture, and corrected me constantly. Richard, the artist who drew strange animals that he insisted he had encountered. One of his creations turned out to be an opossum. We Canadians had never seen one. We thought he'd invented it. Turned out that indeed Richard's opossum was the first of many that made their way across our border.

Paula and Blanca, two beautiful South American women were surprises too. Although there were many blessings and performances of marriage before theirs, one I was honoured to perform in 2001, none of them were made legal. The law was changed much later in Ontario and later still in Canada. The United States took years to catch up.

Their marriage was not a "mistake" or a "technicality." It was a marriage made legal before the law changed. I would argue it was through the power of the Holy Spirit, or *Ruach*, in Hebrew, which is a feminine entity. The women who entered into it were very much in love. Paula and Blanca were non-white, working-class women. There was no media. There was no fanfare. There was simply love, and a congregation of people who had justifiable fear of what might happen to us, yet who still supported the union.

Read their vows: "I take you to be my wife from this moment on. I promise to be true to you in good times and in bad, in sickness and in health. I will love and honour you. I vow to give and receive, to speak and to listen, to inspire and respond, to respect and to cherish, and to work with you to achieve the goals and dreams of our lives." Paula and Blanca wrote those words and they meant them.

We sent the banns application in to the registrar's office. The banns are a way of vetting the marriage through the Church rather than getting a licence at City Hall, which would have been rejected. Clergy can order the banns forms and then use them in place of a marriage licence. To fulfill the banns, Paula and Blanca's names would be read out for two consecutive weeks and if no one objected, then the wedding was on. No one objected. Nowhere on the banns was man or woman mentioned, just groom and bride. Then we prayed and sent the forms in to the Registrar's Office, which mistook Paula for a man's name and vetted the union.

Ruach took over, that feminine face of the Divine. They received their licence, the first in Canadian history, in the mail. Then all hell broke loose. It tends to when Ruach is at work in the world. So, it bears repeating, the first legalized same-sex marriage in Canada was of two racialized women, performed by a woman. Fact.

Women are written out of history constantly. This book is an attempt to write some of them back in. As Muriel Rukeyser said, "What would happen if one woman told the truth about her life? The world would split open?" The #MeToo movement showed, as have others, what might happen if women stand together. The world does split open.

I was the beneficiary of waves of feminisms and womanisms and queernesses. It is a life that would have been impossible to live any other time, in perhaps any other place. Great change changed me. We attempted to let the world split just so the light could shine through.

Thank you to those that shine and have shone. This is yours.

PART I

SURVIVING AND BECOMING

CHAPTER 1
QUEER EVANGELISM AND A LITTLE GIRL

I was raised in a sort of dissolute generational matriarchy. My grandmother had an affair with a neighbour, pre-World War I, producing two of her four children. Grandpa, many years before I was born, had left Grandma for the maid and returned to England. Originally, they'd tried homesteading in Saskatchewan. As a single parent, Grandma then moved to Toronto. Way before women were considered "persons" in Canada, Grandma was, legally speaking, her husband's property. I like to imagine her not only breaking social convention but escaping patriarchy in her own Victorian way. She lived to have another lover, "Chief."

Mother moved her own family home with Grandma in the 1930s, as the Great Depression hit, since my father was out of work. By the time I was born, in 1950, she had followed Grandma's example and had had an affair with the man I called Uncle Ken, who lived with us. Dad, I gathered later, had a whole other family somewhere else.

Men, I was always taught, were a distraction or a luxury, never essential in our homes. I was also to understand this made us not "of this world"—the world of bourgeois convention. Their world would always find us strange. The women who were my role models would have lovers, husbands, and sometimes both at the same time. I was raised in a polyandrous

7

household with two dads. Being queer, being sexually different, wasn't so very queer on Bedford Road.

Okay, there's the queer part, but what about "evangelism"? Neither of the women before me were religious in the least. At best, they'd describe themselves as agnostic. My grandmother's father, my great-granddad, was a Fabian Socialist (I inherited that too). My rebellion against their understanding—all of them—of God as the "opium of the masses" was a revolt against an ideology that seemed every bit as religious as religion, too rote, too unquestioning.

Not that I didn't agree God (as old white male with beard directing human traffic) had no place, but even as a child I found there was something about the Jesus persona that always made sense. He was another rebel against state-sanctioned morality. More than that, I craved the Divine He embodied and the promised land He guaranteed. Surely there was a better, less chaotic place than my family. Surely there should be a land less violent than our world.

However, let it be clearly understood. I loved that my matriarchs raised me as an atheist. I had no toxic religion in my background. The kind of self-hatred many queer friends experienced wasn't part of my experience. My matriarchs raised me to be heretical, modelled ethical heresy, and loved me. That was their holy gift to their grand/daughter.

■

I recall three significant dreams from childhood that speak louder than consciousness about the reality of my home life. I have since learned that although the adults of my childhood, with the exception of my grandmother, said they loved me, their own inner struggles precluded the real care of a child. I was, in many instances, required to be "adult." It was necessary that I be prepared to take charge of chaotic situations, to make decisions beyond any child's ability.

The first dream begins with a shadow walking up the third-floor stairs in our house on Bedford Road to the small middle room where Ken, my "Uncle," slept. I follow the shadow. I'm terrified because it leads me into his room. As I begin to open the door, I wake up.

Ken was the son of Grandma's last known lover, a man who died before I was born. Ken and his then-wife owned an haute couture salon on

Avenue Road. She would do renditions of Parisian dresses that they then sold to wealthy Toronto women. When Ken's wife died, Grandma invited Ken to live with us. We had a few people who rented rooms in the big old house, so on the surface that made sense. By the time I was born, however, Ken was involved with my mother and, for all intents and purposes, served as my stepdad. Except of course for the inconvenient reality of my dad's presence now and then.

Ken was a military man. He'd been among the troops that liberated Auschwitz, or so I was told. Or was it another camp? Often historical details were embellished or changed at Bedford Road. Ken never spoke of it but the whispers around him in adult conversation did. In snooping around his room as children, I saw the grainy black-and-white photographs. Skeletons staring from barracks. Naked hollow people. You remember such moments from childhood.

It was Ken who took me to dance classes. Ken who took us shopping. Ken who drove us up to the family cottage and stayed with us there. Ken who financially supported us. Ken who always arrived at breakfast at the same time. My breakfast was Sugar Crisp, white toast, and milk. His, brown toast and coffee. It was also Ken who, one day as I was slurping down my second bowl of cereal, picked up a knife and slashed my Aunt Lorna across the neck. Aunt Lorna was my mother's sister. I remember feeling as if I were in a dream, immobilized. I watched without being able to act. The randomness of the violence, an unusual side of a man who I thought was so dependable, put me into shock. As I write this, only now do I feel the profound sadness, fear, horror. Would he attack me next?

Crazy Aunt Lorna, we called her. She also lived with us. Lorna, adult whispers informed, had a breakdown when she was thirteen years old and then spent many years in an institution. By the time I came to know her, she was an amusing, slightly batty old woman. Lorna took us to the Canadian National Exhibition every year and would go on all the rides with us. I still remember her on the Rotor, a centrifugal-force cake tin that whirled so fast you stuck to the sides. Lorna stuck to the side with her dress hiked up, exposing the fact that she had baggy underwear the colour of bad weather. Lorna was a truly loving woman whose brain had been damaged by exactly the kind of electro-shock my strange grandfather, her father the Doctor, experimented with.

As a kid, I was horrible to Lorna. Once Graham—my brother from another mother, whom I'll discuss later—and I put salt in her coffee to see if she could tell it wasn't sugar. She couldn't.

Who knew why Ken slashed Aunt Lorna across the neck that particular morning? No doubt she was nattering on about something or other, but she always did. Nothing was very different. There were only the three of us in the kitchen that morning, me, Ken and Lorna. Her blood sprayed in an arc across the linoleum. She didn't scream. Perhaps she was in shock although I wouldn't have known it back then. Was there chaos after? Perhaps. Perhaps I was in shock, too. Was I afraid? Nothing changed. The next day Ken was at the table having breakfast as before. Lorna lived.

My brother Don, the younger of my two brothers, the charismatic, involved brother, called our house "the House of Usher" after Poe's tale of horror. Years later, as my father lay recovering from open-heart surgery, I asked Dad why he stayed with my mother, or at least didn't leave her completely. They clearly hadn't been happy with each other and their yelling and screaming at each other hurt me. He said, "I stayed to take care of you." But he didn't take care of me. It was his own delusion that he was even a main player. The irony escaped him. Really no one was very present.

No one was around on the day Ken didn't come to breakfast either. This time, though, the dream prepared me. Again, Lorna and I were in the kitchen. Again, I was eating toast and Sugar Crisp. Mother never woke much before noon. When Ken didn't arrive, I immediately remembered the dream, and I knew what I must do. It's amazing how perceptive children are. I also knew I needed to take charge. I climbed the stairs to the third floor and his bedroom. No shadow in real life, just me. I knocked on his door. No answer. I knew even before I opened it that something had happened.

Ken was lying in his bed in his pajamas. The top of his head was blown off (I figured that out later). Blood and brains were all over the bed and wall. His teeth were in a glass of disinfectant by the bed. I hadn't known until then that his teeth were false. I didn't scream. I was very calm. I knew I needed to do two things very quickly. One was to say nothing to my mother. The other was to call my big brother, Don, who had been living on his own for some time. He in turn called my cousin, who was a cop. The next few days were filled with adults and commotion. I don't remember the funeral. Much of the few years that followed is very blurry. How old was

I then? Twelve? Thirteen? Fourteen? Somewhere in there. Now there's no one left to ask.

Mom only survived for a few years after Ken's death. Ken had pretty much helped her to live. Dad didn't survive Mom for long, either. They both died in their early sixties. Mom had me when she was forty-five, long after my two older brothers, who were born to her as a teenage bride. I don't remember any of the funerals. Was I kept away? Even Don died young, in his fifties, in 1984. All of them seemed to circle around that Bedford property. Don, who became a minor kind of rock star in the band Lighthouse, couldn't stay away for long. He and his partner ran it as a rooming house long after everyone had died.

I'm now in Ministry at Trinity-St Paul's United Church Centre for Faith, Justice and the Arts, just blocks from the House of Usher on Bedford Road. The Divine is ironic. Full circle. Though I've travelled to ninety-six countries, I haven't been able to stay very far away either. Maybe ghosts are real, and Ken is calling. Just recently I was invited to tour an apartment in that old Victorian childhood home. It's been divided into three luxury condos. The developer did beautiful work. Many of the Victorian touches were carefully preserved even while new kitchens and bathrooms have been added. Any trace of my family and, I hope, any ghosts, have been expunged with the renovation. Good thing.

■

In the second dream, I am being chased home from school by a gaggle of boys. They are taunting me, "Dyke! Lesbo!" I am a fast runner but maybe not fast enough. I'm terrified as they gain on me. I am very young, maybe six or seven, when I first dream this dream. Some of the boys are much older and much faster. I fear the worst. What is the unspecified worst that I fear? In my panic I magically gain speed and suddenly just leave the earth! I'm soaring! I fly without wings, without anything. I am gloriously free. To this day that feeling is one of the very best I've ever experienced. The boys become inconsequential. Little, tiny figures far away. I am free.

Except that in real life I never flew. I simply ran. Every day I ran home from grade school with boys in pursuit yelling "Dyke! Lesbo!" Every day I exploded from the school with the bell or soon thereafter upon seeing them. In the classroom, I was all bravado. I jeered and put down those stupid boys, but I knew I'd pay for it as soon as I lost our adult supervision. The chase was how I paid for it. I was a fast runner in track and field. Though small, I was speedy. If I could get a half-block lead, I knew I could beat them. I was never caught, but I never left the earth either.

Importantly, at the time I had no idea what they meant by *dyke* and *lesbo*. I was clueless. No other children seemed to know either. We just knew these were very bad names and they represented something nasty too. I wasn't cute, and some said I looked like a boy back then. I assumed that's all they meant—ugly. How did they know who I really was? Again, children are perceptive.

Now it seems clearer. Children are culture sponges and we had all imbibed patriarchy from birth. Girls who taunted boys and girls who laughed at boys weren't normal. Those little boys, without knowing it, were the strike force for control over uppity females. Girls who talked back were "dykes." The boys probably didn't know what the words meant either, just that their parents used them.

Hell, I even had a cute little boyfriend back then. He was cool because he wore rubber boots with the tops rolled down. His name was Pasquale. His household was very different from mine. I grew up in a very WASPy home despite my father's last name, DiNovo. The DiNovos had emigrated from Italy at the turn of the twentieth century, when immigration meant dropping your language and assimilating as quickly as possible into the hegemonic culture. We ate Yorkshire pudding and roast beef after the style of my English grandmother, and we called the turkey neck the "pope's nose" in a slur against Roman Catholics. Pasquale was Roman Catholic and had a small glass of wine with dinner. I had already learned that being an outspoken female was undesirable. I also learned that there was something wrong with my last name. How I wished I were a Wilson like Grandma! The bully boys made fun of kids like me with Italian or Jewish last names.

Ironically, exclusion included almost everyone back then. It wasn't until I was an adult that I associated my mother's maiden name, and Gran's married name, Patrick, with the Irish! Obviously, that was something the family didn't want mentioned either. Pasquale wasn't the only difference I encountered at Huron Street Public School. My best friend, Helen Bielawski, was Jewish and invited me to her home on Markham Street to her brother's bar mitzvah. Their home was filled with smoke and piles of money on the table for the new "man." It was another world, filled with singing and candles. Very few guests were speaking English. Her grandparents had numbers on their arms. I didn't ask about them. It never occurred to me that they had anything to do with Ken's black-and-white photographs. Mostly we children lived in a world of mystery even about our own parents and their stories, never mind parents from across the world. We kept to ourselves, our own little reality, and if I remember, we giggled uncontrollably at almost everything.

■

In the third dream, my grandmother is on a large grey horse. Her hair flows down her back, long and white with one blonde streak. As a falconer would hold a falcon, she holds an owl. She loves me.

The dream convinces me of life after death. My grandmother, Helen Wilson Patrick, or Wilson Patrick as she signed her paintings, loved me in life and in dreams and somehow still loves me now. In a household narrative marked by arguing, fighting, and outbursts of violence followed by repression, my grandmother was the one sane presence. Her settler story is emblematic of a generation of Victorian offspring who came to North America escaping old world morals and troubles. She found instead new world morals and troubles. Her husband had wanted adventure. In a way, they were hippies, back to the land people who rejected bourgeois normalcy. Not only did they recreate much of what they had escaped, but they found themselves on inhospitable terrain with little family to rely on.

Helen Wilson Patrick loved England. She loved London. She loved her large family, eleven brothers and sisters in all, most of whom she would never see again. Because of her husband she found herself in the middle of the prairies where brutal winters and loneliness almost drove her mad. Grandma would tell me of days and nights with Grandpa gone, watching the horizon for any potential visitors who were still hours away. She had won prizes as an artist in London. In Lloydminster she was a housewife with four young children and no help. Such was the immigrant story for thousands of women who followed their husbands' dreams.

The land my grandparents were given to farm was Native land, stolen land. The Indigenous People were killed or forcibly moved many years before they arrived. Then, too, my grandmother was property. Before the Persons Case in Canada, women were the property of father then husband. Her neighbours, also settlers, were present when my grandfather was so often absent. The husband next door was helpful, loving. Helen relied on him often, his help on the house and the farm, everything. Her third and fourth children were his, the first two my grandfather's. Did Grandpa know? Did he care? The fact that my mother and one of her brothers were the offspring of some man who lived miles away was never mentioned in their lifetimes. I learned it from an aunt many years later.

Of course, Grandpa wasn't faithful either. Like many men, he had affairs as he travelled. Somewhere or other he picked up a medical licence and morphed his career into providing medical care as the only doctor for miles around. Like much about my grandfather the details are sketchy. How long did it take for a medical licence back then? What did he do for money until it arrived? Was he supported financially by his relatives in England? Now there's no one alive who can answer those questions.

Eventually he left for good, with a woman who had been employed as a servant to help Grandma. He returned to England, a place he had always hated. Helen Wilson Patrick was left in Toronto, a single mother who now couldn't return to her beloved London. Years later my mother and I visited Grandpa's widow in Dover, a sweet old lady in a beautiful house. Helen Wilson Patrick would have loved the house my grandpa died in. She could have had a studio overlooking the ocean.

Locally, Dr. Patrick was known mainly for building one of the first electro-shock machines at the farm (one of my unsuccessful bills in politics was a bill to delist electro-shock from Medicare) and for writing a book on philosophy that some flimflam man promised to get published in New York. The man, the money, and the manuscript disappeared. Photos of Grandpa show a pig-faced, pompous little man, whereas Helen Wilson Patrick was beautiful, even in her old age. As a child I remember her brushing her waist-length hair, with the one golden streak. She was in her eighties at the time.

Grandma refused to ever give Grandpa a divorce. Who knows why? His repentance was to send money for her children from time to time. In Toronto, at least, she could set up a salon and begin to paint again. Portraits in the grand master style were her forte, and I loved to watch both the prominent people and also our family members pose. The smell of oil-based paints still brings her back to me. We all survived, with her and because of her. Tenants and Ken helped.

My father even contributed some money, sometimes. Because he and my mother rarely spoke, just yelled at each other, they would use me as a go-between. "Cheri, ask your father for the money he owes me for March!" Dad had just walked in the door. "Dad, Mommy wants the money you owe her for March." The yelling would begin. I retreated to my room. It was always the same scenario. For us, that was the norm.

Grandma's presence prevented the worst of it or brought it all to an end rapidly in the sweetest, calmest manner. In her own way, though, she was fierce. My image of her is with a cigarette hanging out of the side of her mouth—a "coffin nail," as she called them—with a paintbrush or glass of sherry in her hand. She bequeathed to us the idea that you could be in the world but not of the world. You could find your own out. She ran her studio, or salon, and her rooming house as if she were a grande dame. If you could sing, write, play an instrument, or tell a fantastic tale, you were invited to stay for dinner or even take a room if necessary. Consequently, the house was always busy and we never had fewer than eight for dinner. Those upon whom she bestowed her love were granted every benefit of every doubt. When Ken, terrible narcoleptic driver that he was, ran into a parked car, Grandma said, "What a stupid place to park!" When she loved you, you stayed loved.

Glenn Gould, the great Bach interpreter, came and practised at our house and stayed for dinner. The Royal Conservatory of Music was just down the street. Mostly, though, it was a motley mix of the strange and needy. One "artist" ate toothpaste (which we children found hilarious) and painted like Dalí. Grandma would do classic still lifes and he would turn the same subject matter into the stuff of nightmares. Another woman we children called the "Water Witch" was left to look after me for a week when the family went to visit my uncle and I was still in school. The Water Witch made me scrub the floors, then proceeded to dye all the sheets in the house in the backyard. The dirty dishes were piled to underneath the cabinets by the time the family returned home. When I remember that time, what I find startling is that I blithely went on with my life. Strange as it was, it was in many ways less chaotic and weird than every other week at Bedford Road.

When, for a time, John and Ruth Keene and their son Graham moved in upstairs, Graham and I became co-conspirators and feral brother and sister. We were almost the same age, three or four at the time, but I ruled, as I'd witnessed Grandma do. I was the imperious big sister to Graham, who dutifully did what I told him to. He dressed up in my tights to play the

Prince to my Princess. One day he tied my skipping rope around his neck because I wanted to see if he could hang himself from a railing. Luckily, we were so little and incompetent that we didn't follow it through.

Mostly we ran around downtown on the subway system, in and out of museums and art galleries, which were mainly free to children back then. On weekends we were sent out of the house to play and told to come back for dinner. From the earliest of ages, we walked to school on our own. My running from the boys episodes happened later, after Graham's family bought their own home and moved away. When we were seven or eight we explored Toronto as if it were our private playground. I remember a man asking if we'd like to make $25, a ridiculous amount of money to us then. We giggled and ran on. We assumed he wanted us to steal for him. We knew enough to know there was something wrong in the offer, but had no inkling he was likely a pedophile. One day we took furniture and knick-knacks, anything we could carry, out onto the front lawn of our house to sell. We wanted to buy some games at the Kresge's or Woolworth's around the corner. No one seemed to notice until Ken came home and chased us around the house a few times.

We weren't bad kids, just wild. With Grandma, though, we were perfect angels. No matter what we did, she loved us completely. When we removed price tags from games and switched them for cheaper ones so that we could afford them, we were immediately caught, but she understood that it was because we weren't getting enough allowance. If our parents thought we were wrong, Grandma always "knew" the fault lay with them, not us. In a way she was correct. Our parents were so involved with their own neuroses, they had little time for offspring. We avoided the parents. Anyway, Grandma was the better storyteller.

One night at our cottage when I had to share a bed with her, she told me a story. I found it creepy sleeping with an old woman even if she was my Gran. She sensed that and tried to comfort me. Here was her story:

"When I studied at the Art Institute in London, I met a young man. I'd already met your grandfather and we were not yet engaged, but I knew he was about to pop the question. There was something about the young man though. Something very different. One day after class he asked if he could walk me home. I said yes. I shouldn't have but I did. As we walked, he declared that I was the most beautiful, wonderful woman he had ever known. The young man said I was everything he'd always dreamed of and longed for. I can't say, looking back, that I wasn't flattered and intrigued. Your grandpa never said such things. I told the young man, however, that I was already spoken for. I told him that I loved your grandfather. He looked at me as though I'd hit him. He recoiled. He turned and left me standing there, walking so fast away that he almost ran. I could hear him weeping."

"What happened to him, Grandma?" I was enthralled. I'd forgotten I was sleeping next to an old woman.

"Within the week, after your grandfather formally proposed to me, I heard from a mutual friend that they found the young man hanging in his room. He'd killed himself."

Grandma rolled away and went to sleep. I stared at the ceiling and listened to her snores. I wasn't frightened. I wasn't shocked. I was in awe of her.

My grandmother embodied a great quote from the Belgian comic strip artist Jean-Claude Servais: "The hour calls for optimism. We'll save pessimism for better times."

CHAPTER 2
THE REVOLUTION

K ids. Kids everywhere. The cops on horseback had broken up the anti-Vietnam War rally (I remember a lawyer saying "Get their badge numbers!" to no avail), and the demonstrators streamed into the downtown core. The Anarchists, mostly kids, started smashing store windows. The Maoists, kids too, were waving the Red Book and shouting "Running dogs of U.S. imperialism!" This completely astounded Saturday shoppers, who thought the Maoists were referring to the kids running up the street. That's when someone started yelling, "It's the revolution!"

Instead, and perhaps regrettably, it was just a bunch of us socialist, hippie, peacenik, anarchist street kids. We were a tiny minority at the time in a vast capitalist state. I was a cynic. The Vietnam War was an abomination, no doubt, but the kids I hung out with in the street drug trade never believed for a moment the adult world would change, not really. We all wanted to be William Burroughs or Jimi Hendrix or Janis Joplin. We assumed we would die young. It was far more romantic and more likely than revolution.

I'd left home at fifteen, believing myself to be more mature than the neurotic, violence-prone adults at home. In that I was at least somewhat correct. There wasn't a name for what afflicted me back then, but it's pretty safe to say I suffered at the very least from PTSD. The other children I met on the street were much the same. For most of us it was safer on the streets—couch-surfing, sleeping rough, or piling into a rented room somewhere—than going home. Occasionally, I'd sneak back to the House of Usher to sleep, but it was never worth it. I didn't need my mother harassing me about where I'd been. I'd been everywhere.

I fed myself by selling LSD, at the time under the Food and Drug Act and not criminalized, that was imported from California in hollowed-out Bibles. Yes, I get the irony. The product was so pure and strong that we'd pay $5 each for tablets in quantity and then divide them into four and charge $10 each. A quarter would keep you stoned for twenty-four hours. Despite the excellent profit margin, we never had any money. We were kids and we were also stoners. Try counting money while stoned on acid! We lived on toasted danishes and coffee. Booze was déclassée, and besides, we were way underage. We got stoned almost every day on something, all "soft stuff"—pot, hashish, acid, mushrooms. Someone was always trying to tune a guitar. We listened to music constantly, rock, jazz, and experimental, and we read voraciously. One year I decided to focus on all the French authors available at a local bookstore in alphabetical order, from Artaud to Zola. Doing anything else, like school, seemed such a waste of time. After the last sale of each night we hunkered down with the turntable on and engaged in far-ranging, stoned discussions. Our topics went from revolution to jazz to cinema, and in memory we were all brilliant. Certainly we were precocious and arrogant. Now I look back with nothing but love for those teenagers who knew everything.

Who were we? Some of the group are still alive. There was Gary (whom we called Gary the Jew), Stoned Richard, Japanese Bev, Little Richard (as distinct from Stoned Richard), Faye, Bob, and others. Those are the ones who I know survived. Since then we've scattered across the continent and beyond. At some point each of the boys ended up in prison with absurdly long sentences. While still a teenager, Gary sold an ounce of weed, was busted for trafficking, and got two years. Sexism worked for us girls. Well, it sort of worked. It was assumed we were simply hangers-on to the boys. I remember a car full of narcs, burly plainclothesmen, who told me with slimy rape overtones that "A little girl like you should be careful out on the streets." It was clear to me that authority was definitely not to be trusted. Cops weren't "protectors." They were our enemy. We were disposable, not children but a menace to *their* children. As young women, we were prey. We carried the gazes of old men, including cops, on our bodies. We were objects. The message was overt and had been received. That moment produced in me a suspicion, a distrust of all male authority. I still consider that distrust realistic and healthy.

Sexual liberation meant that we should have sex with men whether we really wanted to or not. Pity fucks, we called them. Friendly fucks. Fucking fucks. The appeal, if there was one, was to be desired, wanted. It wasn't about whether we were having a good time. It was whether the boy was. His good time gave us a measure of "power over," no matter how illusory. I'd always been attracted to both boys and girls, and I learned very quickly girls were more complicated but also more fun.

Sexual assault is so commonplace. In fact, of all the women I've known well enough that they confided in me, I have never met one who has not been sexually assaulted. Somehow, I escaped rape on the streets until much later, in my early twenties. The aggressor was a past lover, a boy whom I considered a friend. I was at his place to collect some of my stuff. It was definitely a power move on his part, an actual assault. His point was to show me clearly that I was simply a "thing." An object. That I was less than human. The assault seemed familiar somehow, as if the world had prepared me for that moment, from the bully boys as a child, to Ken's violence, to most movies and most books. I remember pretending bravado, and after he was done, I laughed at him. I grabbed my stuff and ran. I'd seen all those movies where a man grabs a woman and she melts into his arms. The reality was ugly, no melting. There was no point fighting, you just hope to survive and get the hell out as fast as you could. The boy remained a friend for many years, although living a long way away. We went on as if nothing had occurred. Trauma can be like that.

Decades later I told the story. We happened to be in the same city when I was attending a conference, and we met for coffee at my invitation. I wanted to raise the subject and instead, surprisingly, he did. "So, who was it that you were speaking about?" he asked. *Maclean's* magazine had done an article on women with profile who had been raped. I had been included. I was shocked, intimidated, and I felt the same sensations I had when he assaulted me. In short, his question muted me. I brushed off the question—"Ah, let's not talk about that"—even though that's exactly what

I had wanted to talk about. When I returned home, I sent him an email: "You know as well as I do that I was speaking about you." I had more courage from a distance. I never heard from him again.

As a woman friend said to me, "He probably didn't think he was doing anything wrong." Possibly the most terrifying aspect of rape and the threat of rape is that, in a sense, according to his cultural conditioning, in his own mind, he wasn't doing anything wrong. He was being a man, taking control. He was forceful, aggressive, demanding, successful. In his mind, I "should have" found that maleness arousing, exciting, desirable. My cultural conditioning prepared me to be raped. Women were told to cultivate "desirability." We were taught to attract a man who would want to rape us. In a twisted way, we were told that would give us control. Supposedly, we made it happen. Obviously rape is one of the worst forms of assault, but rape culture is real and affects women as well as men. The paradigm of straight sex, mirrored often in all sex, is a twisted version of the Hegelian master and servant dialectic. Or at least it seemed so.

We girls were well-schooled. We understood our "place," but we didn't like that place. We fought back. Our attitude was a resounding "fuck you!" The second wave of feminism was in full swing. We began to use men the way they used us. We chose women. We wore micro-minis, no bras, and we defied men to say a word. We left them before they could leave us. We laughed in their faces over and over. We got political. When men in cars catcalled me, I went right up and yelled at them. We survived but we still got raped.

Meanwhile, the hallucinations of LSD became tiresome and softer drugs no longer sufficed. A new drug hit our streets, made and sold by our local bike gang. It was methadrine and it changed my life. I realized it was everything I liked about LSD without any of the negatives. No troubling "crazy" moments. Methadrine, or methamphetamine, was just the euphoria and the ability to go without sleep or food. It was cheaper than cocaine and more direct. Like a poster child for a slogan about gateway drugs, I moved from acid to meth. It took some effort. For starters I had to buy it from the bike gang. That meant walking a gauntlet in a coffee shop/ diner filled with bikers. Imagine a teenager who looked about twelve walking past a collection of psychopaths just so she could score. I wasn't going to laugh at *them*. I wasn't "insane." As I said, it took some doing, but I didn't do it for money. I never sold it. Too risky. I just wanted to use.

The experience of "copping" was so hazardous and nasty that it was better to do it infrequently. That meant buying larger amounts, which was not good either. Methadrine also meant needles. It was nasty-tasting and besides, it was the rush that was worth it in and of itself. With a needle there was no waiting for anything. Bang. Stoned. My cousin, son of my uncle the biochemist, was already used to hitting morphine, and was staying at Bedford Road at the time. He taught me how to use a "set of works" with acumen. One time my cousin was hitting me up with meth when my father walked in. Startled, I blurted to my terrified father, "I've been meaning to tell you, Dad, I'm a lesbian," rushing my coming out story to him. Whatever part of my brain that was functional probably thought telling him then would soften the impact.

I wasn't a lesbian, but I didn't really know you could be queer back then. I didn't know you could be bisexual, so lesbian was the word I used because at that time I had a girlfriend. My mom had died. Ken had killed himself. Only Dad was still alive and I can't believe the hell I put him through, that fifties man. I followed up "I'm a lesbian" with "Don't worry, Dad, it's only methadrine, not heroin," as if that made any difference. Later, after his death, we discovered notebooks he'd kept detailing my activites. He'd been following me. Poor, sad dad. He, who had been absent throughout my childhood, was creepily present when I least suspected it. How very "of his generation" to ignore the women in your life until they were "unfaithful," at which point you became obsessive. I simply felt sorry for him.

Just writing about the methadrine days now, decades since I've had anything like it, brings back that glorious experience for that post-traumatic teenage kid. People who are in recovery from addiction will understand when I say that everything I felt was wrong in my life, that drug made right. It's incredible that I'm alive at all. I am profoundly lucky.

I'd like to say it was grace, but one day on Bloor Street, outside the Swiss Chalet near Bedford, I passed out. Hit the pavement. I came to before an ambulance could be called and before too many people gathered. I managed to get myself a chicken sandwich—the best I'd ever had, which was when I realized I hadn't eaten or slept in days. That moment I discovered something in myself that has saved me a few times since. I didn't want to die. Later I slept. It was the best sleep too. With the help of good adults, a psychiatrist who enabled me to get student welfare and a minister at a local shelter, I got back to community college to earn my high school equivalent. I stopped using.

Centennial Community College, with its high school equivalency program, was geared exactly for kids just like me. I'd dropped out after grade ten. The college was populated with kids serving time, kids out on day parole, kids from institutions, and kids like me coming off the streets. Our professors were products of similar stories, or they would have had good university jobs. One was a refugee from the Gulag, another a defrocked priest. They were some of the best teachers I've ever had. We kids were all motivated by the same small voice that reminded us we wanted to stay alive. Hindsight suffuses the entire experience with light and grace. Somehow, in spite of everything, teachers and students alike were free. Freedom is grace, always. We, with grace, had survived. That year was a holy year. We left the college as apostles of survival, mentored by other survivors, knowing it was possible. We learned to love our damaged, fucked-up selves. It was entirely conceivable, for many for the very first time, that we might live.

For our drama project before graduation, we students, under the auspices of faculty, staged the most appropriate play we could find, *Marat/ Sade,* about inmates in an asylum recreating the French Revolution. Most of us in the cast weren't even acting.

CHAPTER 3
TEENAGE TROTSKYIST

A documentary I had watched on the CBC got me to walk into a Trotskyist meeting. It seemed clear to me, even if it wasn't explicit in the film, that capitalism, based on perpetual growth, was incompatible with a healthy earth. If growth meant chewing up resources, and it almost always did, and making money for shareholders meant growth, then sustainability wasn't possible.

Of course, socialism had always been in the air at the House of Usher. My father was an almost full-time volunteer for our Labour Party, first the Co-operative Commonwealth Federation, then the newly formed New Democratic Party (because the CCF made people think "communist"). I had canvassed with him as a kid and held protest signs when George Wallace, a racist southern governor, came to town. Graham and I shoved Conservative Party flyers down an apartment's incinerator because Dad said it was necessary. I learned early what was meant by political expediency.

Even as a teenager, though, I knew that social democracy wasn't enough. The great social democracies, which were admittedly way, way more livable than North America, still offshored their sketchy labour practices and were still capitalist. I believed we needed true socialism, where the larger industries and companies were under community control. The USSR, still alive and well, was clearly an aberration rather than the socialism it pretended to be. It was just another totalitarian country. So, the Canadian Communist Party, despite its free trips to Russia for youth, wasn't an option. That left only Trotskyism.

That's why one Friday night, when they held their forums on various topics, I went to their meeting. I made quite an entrance. You see, I was only months free from my Acid Queen era and I didn't have a clue about the Left's dress code. I sported platform shoes that added about six inches to my height. Also, I wore a sequined jumpsuit over a body stocking that made it look like I was naked underneath, plus two pairs of fake eyelashes and a black "fall," a fake hairpiece that was popular then. I'd been dyeing my hair jet black for some time. I was a sight. I'm sure they thought I was a drag queen, which I would have taken as a compliment.

It was pretty clear, even to me, that I didn't fit in. Everyone was wearing jeans, nondescript shirts or T-shirts with slogans, and Birkenstocks or runners—still the classic leftist garb. Obviously, we didn't frequent the same places. I lived at the queer clubs, where I would have fit right in. They hung out at pubs, where the beer was cheap. They were welcoming, however. From the first, they generously accepted this weird (queer) new person and invited me along for beers. We were encouraged to learn to speak in public, to refine our rhetoric, to overcome any reticence. All skills I kept. Everyone eventually "presented" on a topic of Marxism at the Friday Night Forums, and everyone was expected to rise and comment during other's presentations. It was Politics 101. Of course, the movement needed bodies and voices. We learned to be evangelists, in the sense of recruiting others to the "good news" of Socialism, and for that it was always about growth.

Within weeks I was taught the new code. I also learned that few had actually read *Das Kapital*, a pretty unreadable tome. I had. Wasn't it the necessary entrance ticket if you wanted to become a Marxist? No, most in the movement got their information from a series of pamphlets that outlined our positions on everything. We were part of the Fourth International, I learned, a worldwide group of Trotskyists who took their name from the analysis that said everything was hunky-dory with the Bolshevik revolution until Stalin came along. Stalin represented the Third International. I learned to sell papers. I learned to infiltrate the NDP to try to move it to the left.

One NDP riding association meeting I attended found me and my father in the same room. My father spent all his time at the mic calling for the expulsion of all Trotskyists. Hilarious. I was truly undercover. I worked on the youth group's newspaper and *The Velvet Fist*, a new feminist journal we women invented. One of the co-editors was Alice Klein, later publisher and originator of *NOW* in Toronto. Much later we learned that the RCMP had an agent working on the papers with us. We wouldn't have cared, even back then. We had nothing to hide and the more help the better. It was a supremely practical movement. Practical and yet, of its time, misogynist, homophobic, and racist.

We women were told that when we protested a beauty pageant, we should wear dresses lest the press think we were dykes. That word again. A young comrade was informed that because he was Jewish, he should go to law school. The movement needed a lawyer. One of my friends, a very feminine Black/Asian gay boy, was told his outfits were too bourgeois, too girly. Such were the times. Of course, we women objected. We queers spoke up. Yet we were informed that the revolution was bigger than any of us and that "identity politics" should fall in behind class struggles. As if we weren't part of the class struggle. As if the majority of queers and women aren't working-class. I and the others fell in, however. We adapted.

I moved into a commune with other party members, mostly women. We held consciousness-raising sessions at night à la Mao. During the day we squabbled about who had drunk more than their share of milk. It was all new to a cynical street kid, but the one extremely transferrable skill was sales. I excelled at it. No one sold more newspapers than I did. At one point they sent me to New York to liaise with comrades there. I ended up staying for almost two years, and that time proved awesome. Their demonstrations brought out tens of thousands of supporters, where ours were just thousands. There, the Trotskyist left was composed of many competing factions. "What do you get with three Trotskyists in a room?" the joke went. "Three political parties and a faction."

In New York in the early seventies, not only did the revolution seem more imminent but more necessary. Our flat was a three-storey walk-up on the Lower East Side and our street was patrolled by a bike gang, which was a good thing. Because of them we were safer than on other streets. We didn't get mugged as often, but we always carried $20 with us in case we were. Too little and you might get hurt, but too much you couldn't afford. A guy living downstairs from us was tortured for his old TV set. Cockroaches were everywhere, like ants at a picnic, and when we turned on the water, a yellow stream of something came out. My roommate and lover at the time, Vangie, was a legal secretary who paid the rent and the utilities on our slum. Later, when she visited me in Toronto in our Canadian version of a slum in the Queen and Bathurst area, she was in awe. "You have a tree. You have a backyard!" Yet, despite it all, New York was excitement. The queer scene was huge. Women's clubs held hundreds of half-naked dancing women. Men with beards and long hair wore dresses—radical drag.

Returning home to Toronto brought into focus how much was wrong in my life, with two real turning points. First, when it became apparent that I was queer and proud of it, the other women in my commune accused me of being "male-identified" because I had a girlfriend. Second, the logic of the movement itself escaped me. If revolution was inevitable, then why did we all have to work so hard at making it happen? Naively, I asked my comrades that question over beers one night. The answer: "Because that way, when it happens, we will be at the vanguard of the change. Don't you want to be a leader in that new world?" I was silent but it occurred to me that argument didn't explain the sad end of Trotsky, our patron saint.

Anarchist friends also made a point. Trotsky brutally ended the Kronstadt rebellion of sailors, not to mention his summary executions of grumbling and starving Red Army soldiers. "The revolution is not a tea party," Mao said. No doubt. My cynicism returned.

Speaking of Mao, however, I can't leave my Trotskyist time without mentioning the Maoists in Toronto. They were mainly the offspring of true bourgeois, and all-white at the time. I met one of them putting up posters. I asked how they expected Chinese immigrants to read them if all the posters were in English. The young blonde Maoist replied, "The language of the proletariat is universal!"

CHAPTER 4

GETTING KICKED ON ROUTE 66

While still in my teens, before joining the Young Socialists, my then-boyfriend Bob and I decided that even though we'd missed the summer of love in 1967 we should still hitchhike to San Francisco, epicentre of all things sixties. So, in 1968, we did. It was a nice break from the streets of Toronto. We had the address of "Little Richard," who'd moved there and would surely put us up. Now that I have children of my own, the idea of having a couple of 17-year-olds hitchhiking across the United States with little to no money is horrifying. Never mind, we had the immortality of youth. Or, God looks after fools and drunks and stoner teenagers.

Our first stop was New York, though not the first time I'd been there. We arrived in the midst of a garbage strike and the city was disgusting. Junkies lay on the street the way only a few drunks did in Toronto. The place where we stayed was dirty and dismal and frightening. Yes, but the shoes were fantastic! I remember spending most of my money on a pair of shoes before we picked up a ride out of there.

It was a memorable trip and so of its time that some of the details are worth noting. Certainly, many of our rides were. One of them was a psychotic Republican who drove us off course into the middle of a forest and then ranted that "you hippies" were taking down his country. Fortunately, he then continued on and dropped us off without killing us. Another was a group of drunk and stoned kids who were mocking a deaf girl in the back seat with jeers of "Don't worry, she's fuckin' deaf. No harm. No foul." On our way home, some rednecks followed us in their car, threatening to run us off the road outside of Winnipeg. That was, of all of them, the most terrifying. I remember thinking we'd survived hitching through the States only to meet our deaths in Canada. The irony. Again, we managed to escape.

There were angels too, like the guys who picked us up as we were arriving in San Luis Obispo. They'd lost all their money in Vegas but put us up in their billiard hall bar anyway and treated us to food and laughter. Or the cops in San Francisco who, unlike our own cops, warned kids about bad acid on loudspeakers from their cop cars. And the angel who, once we arrived in San Francisco penniless and found out, surprise, surprise, that Little Richard didn't live at that address anymore, had us walk along a street where, miraculously, Little Richard was sitting in a diner, hence, giving us a place to crash.

San Francisco, à la New York, wasn't anything like what we expected. Not unlike the sixties themselves, it was not so much peace and love as drugs and depression. We were there on the Fourth of July, Independence Day, when we quickly discovered that you couldn't tell gunfire from cherry bombs. Like my personal journey from acid to methadrine, San Francisco had moved from pot to junk. That was almost as obvious as it was in New York. Still, outside the city the highways were full of kids just like us, from all over North America and all over the world, hoping to find the promised land in California.

One of my most amusing memories, though, was hitching through Texas past the ranch belonging to LBJ, the then-President, a ranch that went on and on for miles. The heat was astounding, very dry. At a gas station I used the restroom and wiped a streak of dirt from my face. On the wall was some grafitti: "Texans you can't shit here your asshole's in Washington." Indeed. By the time we made it back to Canada, we were happy to be home.

My boyfriend Bob survived as well and continued to hitch across Europe when we broke up, picking up some leatherworking skills as he travelled. He landed in Australia and opened a leather hat store that shipped all over the world. Now as "Jack" he calls every so often and tells me of his life in an Australian twang. We were and are beyond lucky.

∎

Back to socialist politics. The simple reality was that my activism never really stopped from that point on. It just took a detour into queer politics. After the paternalistic response to feminism and radical queerness coming from the leadership of the Trotskyists, we needed to find a home where we could be revolutionary, queer, and women. Coming from our socialist backgrounds, we young radicals, although we respected it, found the mainstream gay lobbying a little too polite, our Community Homophile Association a little too mainstream.

We crafted a "We Demand" statement outlining our demands for equality (see the complete statement in Chapter 18). We did this because at the time there were no queer rights. You could be fired, not hired, refused housing, denied benefits, not allowed to marry, or adopt children, all because you were gay. It's difficult to imagine the courage it took to "come out" in public, signing our names to a document demanding equal rights back then. We presented it at the first demonstration for gay rights, held in 1971 in Ottawa on Parliament Hill, and although I was the only woman who signed it, I didn't actually get to the demonstration. I had a test at school. The photos are all of boys.

The first Pride gathering was that same year. It wasn't a parade but a picnic at Hanlan's Point on the Toronto Islands. Hanlan's Point was notorious as a queer cruising ground. A picture of me and my girlfriend of the time was captured by the local gay rights publication. We were "Out" and "Proud." I was so used to being fringe by that point that being queer and out was normal for me.

Michael Hoo, my best friend once I left the Young Socialists, and I shared an apartment. He was the one that was too "girly," too "bourgeois" for the homophobic men and women in the movement. Michael was Jamaican, Asian/Black. He would always say, "The black in me, honey, comes out in all the right places!" We shared entrances. Mine, into the hall on Queen Street at my first Friday night forum wearing sequins. His, getting off the plane in Toronto from Kingston wearing a satin jumpsuit. In Kingston his life had been threatened. Toronto was safer, even then.

Our apartment was the first nice place I'd lived in. Michael had decorated it in mid-century modern furniture. We had a one-bedroom in one of Toronto's first high-rises, in St. Jamestown on Wellesley Street. Our sheets were mustard-coloured. That apartment was timeless design—it would still look good today. If one of us had a lover, they got the bedroom, the other the couch. In the pre-AIDS days, sex was the drug. Michael went out cruising every night. "Know their names? Darlin', sometimes I don't even see their faces!" By day, I held odd jobs. Michael thieved. One day he brought home a seven-foot palm on a trolley. He'd simply walked into the lobby of an office building with the trolley and told the receptionist he'd been ordered to move it, then brought it home. One day I came home to an exquisite little Egyptian bird in the bathroom. Where did it come from? "The museum, dearest, cut the glass like they do in the movies, and moved it." I was just a little horrified and made him promise not to do that again. That was, after all, the people's property. I don't know whether the museum ever regained it. Michael moved out and took his belongings with him. Eventually he was arrested for walking out of a high-end women's store with two fur coats over his arm, and barely escaped deportation.

Our nights were spent clubbing again. Life had returned to fun after days selling newspapers and being chastised for being too male. Capitalism is unrelenting, though. We needed to work. Michael needed to stop robbing. His boyfriend helped. He was a medical student from a wealthy family, one that was right-wing Christian. As far in the closet as one could be, Michael's lover was also engaged to some poor unsuspecting girl. When Michael discovered that, fur flew. Michael threatened to "out" him to his fiancée, his family, his school, everyone. One of his threats was to appear at the wedding dressed as the wicked Queen from *Sleeping Beauty*. Instead he simply got stoned and stayed home. Michael wasn't the only one unlucky in love.

I was seeing a girlfriend, Wanda, who also lived with another woman. She was the first person I knew intimately to have a complete breakdown. She was an MDA dealer—MDA being the precursor to ecstasy—and her apartment was in the same building as ours. She proved you could be funny and smart and still lose it. Her girlfriend had her "formed," or committed, when my Wanda started to hear voices coming out of the radio. Our cool, hip, modern high-rise was beginning to feel more like a high-rise ghetto. The police had raided her apartment at least once. We weren't Rochdale, Toronto's notorious "college" that morphed quickly into a biker-run dealers' space, but we were getting there.

I knew the trend. I had been with the group of adults who planned Rochdale to be the first university where marks wouldn't matter and where peace and love would guide its pedagogy. It seemed flaky to me, the cynical street-kid dealer, and sadly it was. One "class" I remembered attending was some Guru from the East who kept us all waiting for an hour, came in, sat down, said one word, "Love," and then left. At least there were no fees. I stayed away shortly after that. I was trying not to do methadrine and Rochdale was all about methadrine.

St. Jamestown was showing the signs of becoming a Rochdale and Michael and I decided to pack it in and move out. I lost track of him after that but assumed he'd died. I looked for his name on the AIDS memorial in the park next to the 519, the Queer Community Centre, but it wasn't there. Most of the queer men I knew from that era disappeared or died. I often wonder what happened to the med student and his bride. I hold them all in prayer.

There was never a place back then to be bisexual. No one believed in bisexuality. Most still don't. Even though the *B* became part of the LGBTQ2S acronym, it never was part of the reality. Claiming you were bisexual simply meant that you were still in the closet and didn't have the courage to emerge from it. Still sort of does. Later it meant that you were really straight and just trying to be cool. Either way you were effaced. You didn't exist as you. Funny thing though, I existed. So did and do others. At a recent forum on the Year of the Bisexual (so-proclaimed in 2018), I was astounded to see so many people I thought were gay, lesbian, or straight. I said to the room, "It's so gratifying to see a room full of people like me who don't actually exist!"

A professor at seminary once said to me, "I understand gay or lesbian or transgender, but I can't fathom bisexuality. Faithfulness is important." Because clearly we don't exist and we're incapable of monogamy. We must be faithless. I could have spoken to him about the difference between polyamory and bisexuality or about the biblical basis for both, but it really wasn't worth it. When we look back at it, the queer movement, like the Young Socialist movement, was really primarily about the rights of white men. Just as feminism had to grow up and admit its racism and transphobia, so the queer rights movement has had to be dragged by two-spirited, racialized women, bisexuals, trans, and non-binary people into a new era. Needless to say, *intersectionality* wasn't a word in the 1970s.

By the time HIV and AIDS became the word in the early eighties, I was married with children and work. The reaction of governments and agencies was so vile and phobic that any other issue but that pandemic became less important. Important was the simple recognition that queers were human and needed to survive. Not until it became clear that straight people could die, too, did change begin. The men I knew were terrified. We all were. Like street days, some survived, some didn't. Brutal luck again.

I had previously managed to get myself into university from the transition year at community college. The small inheritance I received when my parents died, after the fall of the House of Usher, paid my tuition (which was cheap back then in any event) and rent. Food and essentials, I paid for with a series of low-paid jobs. One of the oddest was a babysitting position I had with a wealthy couple.

I'd been cleaning houses part-time, a relatively easy gig, and responded to a call from a ravine-side mansion. The woman who interviewed me asked if I'd consider watching her three boys instead of cleaning her house. I responded that I'd be delighted to, except, in my experience, cleaning paid more. "Nonsense," she said. "I'll pay your rate." I was in. As nanny after school and for extended periods when the adults travelled, I entered a new world I called "The Discreet Charm of the Bourgeoisie" after Luis Buñuel's great film.

First off, I loved the boys, who ranged from seven to sixteen. They were smart, funny kids. My own dysfunctional House of Usher upbringing came in handy after I discovered the plethora of drugs in the parents' bathroom. The dad was in the medical field and the mother a writer. His preference was "downers," hers "uppers," and in doses that would have fetched a small fortune on the streets. It felt dangerous for me to be around it, but I refrained. When his use became problematic, I recognized all the signs. Slurred speech, coffee everywhere, in his pajamas at noon. The dad was quietly sent to rehab. Who knew there were top secret rehabs for powerful men like him?

I learned from the eldest child to believe the very young. You'd think with my past I would have known that. The eldest son, I'll call him John, came home bragging about his affair with an older woman. Now, bragging about sex goes with the territory of being a sixteen-year-old male, but it was the older woman in question who made this different. None other than Xaviera Hollander, also known as the Happy Hooker. She was famous throughout North America as a sex worker who wrote columns, made appearances and, in Toronto, danced at the same clubs I went to. I had actually thought she was into women. Again, the B for bisexuality is silent.

John said he met her at his retail job, and she'd asked him out. His brothers thought he was insane and had made the entire incident up. All his prep school buddies did too. Bets were made and I, the "responsible" adult, worried about how he'd make this all go away when the truth came out. No one expected that he'd keep the ruse going until the night she was supposed to arrive at the house. But he did. We waited in the living room, fearing for his sanity, the boys and the babysitter. That's when the doorbell rang and Xaviera walked in.

We were stunned. He, on the other hand, having collected a fair wad of cash, disappeared with Xaviera upstairs. Luckily he had the common sense to spend the time simply talking to her, as everyone downstairs was listening intently. I felt conflicted. He was legally of age. She was twice his age at least. It was creepy, but what should I do? Xaviera, strange person that she was, ignored me and the others and later flounced out as casually as she had flounced in. I was "the help." She didn't acknowledge or remember me when I next saw her at a club.

In another scene from the same babysitting gig, a street friend of mine dropped by, asking for help. He'd returned from South America seconds before a coup, and he wanted to quickly sell the cocaine he'd brought with him so he could set himself up in Toronto. Did I know any buyers? I explained I was caring for children, back at college, not in the scene anymore. As he left, so did a tricked-out Lincoln Continental, with two guys who looked like Curtis Mayfield. That street, I'm sure, had never seen anything like it.

It was a memorable job. The most memorable of all was leaving it. To nannies of the world, you have nothing to lose but your children. I loved those boys as if they were mine, feared for them, especially in that household, and missed them when I left. There was nowhere to go with all of that but home and have children of my own. Which I did.

CHAPTER 5

QUE(E)RYING PARENTHOOD

Don and I married precisely because we wanted a child, or, at least, I wanted a child, and he wanted me and went along with it all. He was a draft resister I'd met in a bar. Don was funny, smart, talented. He did political cartoons for a major daily and album covers for local bands. Queer coupling, in my case as a bisexual queer, was something Don and I entered into with eyes wide open. Our wedding vows included a rant against monogamy and the state. Hilarious in retrospect and so very seventies, we meant it more than we knew consciously at the time. I'd never witnessed a happy marriage, at least not one I was intimate enough with to really know. Neither Don nor I had any models to look to. The term "open marriage" was around but meant for us a kind of gross swinger scene. That's not what we wanted. We simply decided we wanted transparency and honesty. We understood that at least two people were needed to raise a child, and we were in the throes of a passionate romance. Francesca was born July 10, 1977.

I'd left university at that point and found myself a job in what we affectionately called the headhunting industry. Or, as a socialist friend called it, "pimping for capitalism." The reality was we needed the money, and God knew I was good at sales. I liked the all-woman environment in the firm I joined. The upside was, at its best, we were helping many women who wanted to make money and stay independent just like us. Don, my new husband, was doing a typesetting apprenticeship that would eventually lead to union work. Since I planned on getting pregnant and taking time off, it was necessary to cover food and rent. Having a job meant maternity leave. Just what corporate men feared, I thought, smiling.

To prepare for the birth, I read everything about childbirth I could and took Lamaze classes. I was the youngest by far in my own family and hadn't been around babies, never mind birth. I had no clue. Lamaze taught us that the correct term for labour was just that, *labour*. We were not to use *pain* since it was simply hard work. I was determined to have a natural childbirth with no drugs, so it was reassuring to learn that this was all about the correct breathing techniques. We found a doctor who seemed open to it and we were both supremely confident that not only would we show the world by having a perfect birth, but we'd have a perfect baby and be as perfect as possible parents. Not like our own parents, God forbid!

The day Francesca decided to be born, I was doing well until it started to hurt. Naively, I had actually believed it wasn't going to! The pain was excruciating, and it was pain. The training I'd really needed was how to deal with pain, not hard work. The messaging I'd needed was that pain was normal and then how to deal with it. No slur against Lamaze, but my naivety was perhaps on a level not suited to their technique. So, because of the pain, I thought something was going wrong. I kept asking the nurse, "How much longer?" The correct answer would have been, "Just try one more contraction." Instead the answer I received was, "There's no way of knowing." Wrong, for me.

Hours later and after constant offers of drugs, I relented. My only thought by then was *make this stop*. Just as Francesca was crowning, the epidural kicked in, necessitating a forceps delivery. Exactly what I hadn't wanted. No matter, the result was a beautiful baby girl. We were ecstatic. That was until we arrived home.

By that point in my life I'd been traumatized, addicted, raped, and homeless on the streets, but nothing prepared me for the horrors of parenting a colicky infant. "Horrors" is not an exaggeration. I felt there was a great patriarchal conspiracy, in which women were criminally complicit, that made of babies God's gifts. No one prepared me or us for this. Then again, how could they? Should someone have told me, as Don's mother eventually did since his sister was also colicky, that I wouldn't sleep for months? Had someone mentioned that I would effectively be imprisoned at home, because where could I have gone with a screaming infant? That at one point I would have prayed for a complete breakdown, but then realized even that would be an unaffordable luxury, since who would look after the baby? Should anyone have said I would be so shaken, thinking she was dying at times, that Don would have to call La Leche League for help with me sobbing in the background? Or that no one would babysit a screaming baby? Or that, returning from my one postpartum visit to the doctor, I could hear Francesca screaming from the street? (My brother and his partner had offered to look after her. They never did again.) If they had, I still would have had her. The irony of parenthood.

The only thing that would calm her at all was loud blues with a thumping bass cranked up to the point that the downstairs neighbours complained. Even then, with loud blues, I would have to dance with her for hours before she'd pass out. The only thing that made me feel blessed was hearing about the death of another baby. It could be worse.

Another woman told me about having colicky twins! She lived in a suburban subdivision and would strap them into her car and just drive all night without stopping at any of the stop signs. If she stopped the kids would wake up. If stopped by the cops, she told me, she planned on handing car and kids over to the cop and going home. After hearing her tale, it made me want to get a car. There was no way around it for either of us. I was responsible for this child forever. No doubt I loved her. Survivor that I was, I survived. After many months the colic subsided. I finally knew what it was to be completely adult. I learned under fire, having responsibility for another.

The older my children got, the easier it became. Her brother, Damien, a happy accident, proved to be placid and easygoing by comparison and only became demanding as a toddler. Don't get me wrong. I love all children, babies and my own, but I wouldn't wish parenthood on the weak. Someone needs to tell young women the truth. Years later, when a congregant had a colicky baby, both Francesca and I helped babysit. It was fun for us because we got to give the baby back.

At any rate, there was no question, having spent that terrible time in an upstairs apartment with no laundry facilities, washing clothes every day in the bathtub: it was time to move. The small inheritance helped. I still had some money left, and we scraped together the down payment on a house. We also bought a Lada, the cheapest car on the market, whose Soviet state-of-the-art mechanics meant the wrench that came with it never worked and the jack split in two the first time a tire needed changing. At least I didn't have to walk to the supermarket with a screaming child strapped to my back.

When Francesca turned two, we enrolled her in a daycare and I returned to work. It didn't last long. After all, I understood that having a corporation take 80 percent of my commissions was exploitation. Why shouldn't I keep 100 percent? I was doing all the work. The clients were mine, and I'd kept them and cultivated them over a few years. I decided to create my own firm and I hoped my clients would follow me. I borrowed $5,000 from the bank and rented some shared space.

About a week before I planned to leave the firm, my manager called me into her office in a secretive sort of way. My immediate thought was "They know! I'm about to be fired." I wasn't quite ready and the prospect of being goose-stepped out of the building carrying a bankers box with photos and pens was scary. Instead, she sat me down and then invited another consultant in. "I'm sorry I wasn't completely forthcoming," she said, peering over her manicured hands. "I need you to witness me firing Jim [not really his name]. He's planning on starting his own firm in contravention of our agreement." So I did. Then rushed across the street to have a quick glass or three of wine.

In fact, my former colleague's firing and successful fight against the non-compete clause in our agreement made it even easier for me to leave later on. Capitalism is a wondrous beast. With my $5,000 dollar loan, I billed $500,000 in my first year with little more than a desk and a phone. I've never come close to making that kind of money ever again. Within a year or two, we were selling our house to move to a 3,500-square-foot dream home in the suburbs.

This queer, socialist kid found herself quintessentially petite-bourgeois, and bizarrely enough we had become, without really planning it, the stereotypical nuclear family. It's almost as if a sign had popped out, some omniscient cartoon balloon saying, "Welcome to the eighties!"

CHAPTER 6
CASINO CAPITALISM

To understand the eighties, one really needs to understand cocaine. Cocaine fueled the eighties. It was expensive enough to make you believe you weren't really a drug user like those other drug users, yet cheap enough to be plentiful in everyone's lives and, of course, make you a drug user exactly like those others. Cocaine didn't give you pesky hallucinations or mystical experiences. It didn't even shift your focus on the world in a way that might lead to questioning what you were doing and what was happening around you. It just made you feel powerful, able, energetic, and more, not less, functional. On cocaine, you didn't need to sleep or eat (you lost weight—a good thing for most!), and you could work, work, work. It was the perfect complement to capitalism.

To the extent that capitalism is a sort of money addiction, it has always been fueled by something. But that era stood out. The revolutions of the earlier eras had failed. Where was the world Marx predicted? Certainly not in the Soviet Union or China. We socialists knew capitalism was doomed or would doom us, but without a revolution on the horizon, we were like the person at the slot machine; we kept pulling the lever. When one of us got lucky, as I did, it was often difficult to not take it personally. I knew it was luck, privilege, and yes, hard work and some smarts. Didn't the factory worker work as hard? Wasn't the street hustler in the ghetto as street smart? We knew we were all in a casino and it taught us humility and the knowledge that it couldn't last. When the Students for a Democratic Society mostly ended up on Wall Street, no one was surprised. Street skills equalled movement skills equalled business skills. It was that obvious. It was all about marketing and sales. Or as a friend said, "It was all bullshit." Like the person at the slot machine, though, cocaine helped keep you awake.

As stated, I started with a $5,000 loan, a desk, and a phone. Following the time-honoured tradition of leaving a larger company hoping my clients would follow me, it worked. Unlike the corporate environment I had left behind, the women who worked for me kept 50 percent of everything they billed. It was a generous step up from the pittance any of us had made working for the Man. Business was good. The two women who worked for me made six figures easily. We didn't care if we stayed small. I was earning more money than I'd ever earned before or have earned since.

As "corporate pimps" we placed mainly women in communications, advertising, public relations jobs, and anything else that would pay us a commission. Not just women. We had a standing order for young preppy university grads who looked and spoke well (of either gender) for a large brokerage firm. They started in the mail room, took courses, and worked their way up. In my firm, I could start really early and leave at 3 in the afternoon to be home when the kids got home from school, leaving the evening shift to the woman who was single and didn't want to wake up until noon.

The little two-bedroom house we'd bought in the late seventies had more than doubled in value in five years. We sold it and bought our dream house in the suburbs, 3,500 square feet sitting on a quarter-acre. The first thing we did was install a pool. My company moved from working at home to digs in the belly of the beast, in the heart of the financial district at King and University. One of our successful placements was my husband Don, whom we found a job as Type Director for a large multinational ad firm. He loved the job and it paid way better than his typesetting gig. Moving on up.

There's a kind of buzz to financial districts. Cocaine again, in part. We could feel it in the air. There was a crazy exhilaration to days when the market is booming and "tale of the dragon" industries like ours are cashing in. I remember a joke I shared at a client luncheon that sounds sad, and has ever since the eighties. "A man walks into a corporate office and the receptionist is asleep at the front desk. He raises his voice to try and wake her to no avail. Finally, he tries to shake her arm. At that moment a manager comes running from the back office screaming, 'Don't wake her, please. She might leave!'"

There was virtually no unemployment. Minimum wage in practice was as high in the eighties as it was thirty years later. Women were climbing the earnings ladder because there simply weren't enough men to hire. Even racialized people were getting decent jobs, although racism was rampant. Large multinational companies would ask for "only good-looking women" or "no non-whites on the corporate floor." We warned them such talk was illegal, but we also knew our warning wouldn't change their hiring.

■

Cocaine may have been the fuel of capitalism. It may have felt harmless—positive, in fact. It was certainly at every party and in every bar downtown. Like capitalism itself, though, it was a not-so-subtle lie. It was addictive. It did harm you. Ultimately it made you less productive, even incapacitated. I wasn't immune, but with two small children and my checkered history with speed, I rarely partook. Others weren't so lucky. Everyone knew someone who lost a job, disappeared, or entered rehab. Excess was the sign of the times. Excess and a very death-like sense of humour. Brokers who worked non-stop were always the ones to generate the viral jokes. One that epitomized the times came to us within minutes of the NASA Challenger crash: "What does NASA stand for? Need another seven astronauts." The market had no compassion. It seemed to all of us that the reality we were experiencing with ever-rising earnings and never-ending profitability would last forever. Even as socialists, we were getting suckered.

I branched into a sideline business, leasing and then time-sharing a box at our largest and newest sports arena. It was a venture with the husband of one of my co-workers, a baseball fan. He would do the day-to-day running and I would do sales to some of the client companies we already did business with. It too was a success.

Despite it all, we still put up our New Democratic Party sign on our front lawn at election time. We were the only ones in our vast wealthy subdivision to do so. The street kid in me was always amazed that what we were able to accomplish in business was legal. In many ways it was far easier, less risky and, of course, vastly more profitable, than drug dealing. I still considered myself a socialist. We were still, in the great scheme of things, petite-bourgeois. At least our business helped our applicants do a little better at the capitalist casino. The crumbs our enterprise made in comparison to the large companies we often dealt with exposed the whole unfair game for what it was. I still have endless respect and a bit of nostalgia for those who run small businesses. They generate 85 percent of the new jobs and they risk everything. The "big boys" clear them out as needed. That's what recessions are for. That, and depressing wages. I should have seen the depression of the early nineties coming. None but the big boys did, though.

I remember the exact moment when the party ended. It was 1990. Don and I and another couple had taken a weekend without kids to go to Key West. There is something poetic about the fact that as my world shifted, we found ourselves in Key West, the entry point for much of the cocaine in North America. Key West was a town flooded with cash. No one took credit or debit there. Why would you in a town awash in cash that needed to be laundered? We kept going to ATMs.

I kept hitting the phone. You see, I had a major deal that was supposed to close at any moment. It was an order from a multinational publishing company for a chief financial officer and our candidate was the top contender. He'd been through multiple interviews and we were just waiting for them to sign the contract. It was a sure thing, but I still needed to be in touch. I should have known when they became strangely difficult to reach. All of a sudden you could feel it, especially in a town like Key West. The financial world shifted. The market news had been grim, but we didn't take much notice of the market. The market was our clients' problem, not ours. That weekend it became my problem. Welcome to the nineties.

Socialist that I was, I should have known the good times wouldn't last. Recessions happen routinely. They're built into the system. It's a fabrication that capitalism thrives on competition. It doesn't. It thrives on consolidation. The rich get richer. The poor get poorer. The middle class empties out. Or at least it had since the Reagan/Thatcher neo-liberal era. The game is rigged. We little players were cutting into the bottom line. Employees were demanding decent salaries and there were too few of them to go around. The unemployment figures were too low. Time to clear the decks.

The publishing firm I was waiting to hear from was a branch plant. When I finally heard from the CEO, he put it succinctly: "We're being consolidated and they're closing this office. Hell, I may not have a job by the end of the week." Many sorries and a profoundly disappointed applicant later, not to mention thousands in lost commissions, I knew the boom was over. Not just for that firm and that applicant, but for us. Like the morning after the wild cocaine-coloured parties, the hangover was ugly.

Certainly, the whole street was freaking out as I returned. No one was hiring. Many of our clients who did business with the same big companies were hearing the same bad news. No one was buying anymore. Advertising was moving in-house. Middle management, our forte, was being eliminated. Drudge jobs that at least provided many, particularly women, with employment were being automated or farmed out to developing countries. The computer era had begun in earnest. Turns out the fax machines and computers that had made our occupations easier also made it easier to do without any of us entirely, or at least easier to replace us with cheaper alternatives.

I faced the grim prospect of starting over, going back into sales, which I hadn't had to do for years, to work twice as hard for half as much. We sold our sports box business for $1 to someone willing to take on the debt. No one was interested in investing in anything. No one was interested in entertaining clients anymore and if they were, they wanted to pay half as much as they had before. Vendors took the hit. I could have survived—that's what I'd always done—but something else was happening in my life. We'd become active in a church. Maybe cocaine entered into that first, too. I'd never forgotten methadrine and how easy it was to live for a drug. Business, money, even being on the dragon's tail of capitalism had been the same sort of exhilaration, the same sort of high. To me, the recession of the early nineties was like the moment I passed out on Bloor Street in the seventies—reality breaking through the fantasy. Without the recession, would I ever have changed? I started going to church before the recession, but I never really immersed myself in church until after. Cocaine left the lives of everyone I knew, and direct involvement in capitalism left mine.

What, though!? Both Don and I were atheists and would never have walked into any faith institution but for an important historical detail, the first Iraq invasion. I'd stayed away from activism of the overt order, but when the bombs started dropping and some of my right-wing neighbours started cheering, we knew we had to act. Don, the draft resister, me, the socialist. What to do? How to do it? The unlikely answer in our suburb was a speakers' series hosted by our local United Church featuring imams, rabbis, and clergy speaking about the concept of a "just war." Was the Iraq invasion a just war?

We went, and honestly, not only because of the war. My son, Damien, had pointed to a neon cross and asked what the "lighted T" was for. I thought, *How are my children going to be able to read Shakespeare or any of the Western literary canon if they don't know something about the Bible?* No public school covered that anymore. What place of faith would teach them the stories without also being homophobic and misogynist? I knew that just recently, in 1988, the United Church of Canada had begun ordaining lesbians and gays who had partners and weren't celibate. So, the Iraq war, my child, and an inclusive policy took us there.

Needless to say, it was also my own spiritual struggle. I took us there when we were making money easily, because something was nagging at my soul. Why did my life revolve around my company's billings? Why was I happy only when we were doing well financially? How was that a way to live? The nineties called everything into question.

CHAPTER 7
AN ATHEIST GOES TO CHURCH

had no idea what went on in church or any faith community for that matter. All I knew was that Richmond Hill United was for the ordination of queers like me and against an imperialist war. Even today, if I find myself in another city looking to worship in a local church, I look for similar markers: pro same-sex marriage, anti-war. I've never been disappointed in finding such a church anywhere in the world. The Christian Right (which is neither) gets the press, but there has always been an alternative.

On our first visit to Richmond Hill United, neither Don nor I knew when to stand or sit. We didn't know the hymns or if we should go up for communion. Church was a strange country. We liked the minister, and the children went off somewhere to Sunday School, so that was relaxing. The children would learn the stories, and perhaps, just perhaps, I'd figure out how to be happy again. Nothing in what we heard seemed too objectionable although neither of us believed in God. It was all strange.

By God, we thought we meant an anthropomorphic monster, creator of the cosmos, who demanded subservience amongst His followers and punished those who didn't comply. Who in their right mind would believe in or want to worship someone like that? Don and I enrolled in a new members' class where we read that we didn't have to believe everything in the Bible literally to call ourselves Christians. We also learned that you

could be queer and faithful. Good stuff, all, but it evaded the central question of God.

Ken, the minister, put it well during an intro to Christianity class,
summing up where Don and I were at. "Cheri is an atheist who doesn't
believe in God but does believe Jesus was God's son. And Don the atheist
doesn't believe in God but does believe Mary was God's mother!" Too true.
For me, there was something about the person of Jesus dying on the cross
who was still able to turn to the dying thief next to Him and offer comfort, saying they would be together in Paradise. I thought it was fiction, but
even so, who could make up something like that? If it wasn't fiction, what
manner of human could say something like that? Who could offer that
glorious lie just to make a stranger feel better before death? What manner
of person was that?

I hadn't heard of Karl Barth then. I hadn't read his idea that "the Bible
is far too important to be taken literally." Barth defended Christianity
from the inside out, clarifying the radicality of a God de-centred, as person, as dying, as fragmented, using the Bible as it was, rather than acting as
a classic apologist. I'd heard of Martin Luther but not his great punk rock
theological statements, like "the Bible is the swaddling cloth in which I lay
my Christ" or "sin boldly and love Christ more boldly still." All I knew
was that something in that weird book intrigued me. I was introduced to
that by a Rolling Stones rendition of a Blues spiritual written by Reverend
Robert Wilkins. "Well, father said, 'See my son coming home to me /
Coming home to me / Father ran and fell down on his knees / Said 'Sing
and praise, Lord have mercy on me.'"

Who was this, falling down on his knees to welcome back a son who'd
wasted his father's money and his own life? A son who treated his father
like an ATM and really was returning just for a free meal. Falling down
on his knees before the son had said a single word. A father who was so
in love with the son that he didn't care. So, God's love was like that, profoundly loving, forgiving anything, delighted just to be with the child She/
He loved. If God, whether noun or verb, wasn't a monster but the very
essence and origin of love, wasn't that something I might believe in or at
least hope for?

I learned early on at Richmond Hill United Church, in actually reading the Bible, that it says exactly that in 1 John 4:16. "Whoever lives in love,
lives in God and God lives in them." God equals love. That made sense. At

least it made enough sense to keep returning to church to find out more. The other equally important aspect of church was the community. I'd never been a part of a community whose sole function was to try and love one another. Every community I'd been a part of had some ulterior motive. It was making a revolution or making money or sharing an identity. In those communities we were endlessly substitutable. The end goal was the real purpose, even if the end goal, as in being queer, was us against them. Eventually, I was baptized. Who could have seen that coming?

Our minister, Ken, became a friend. He asked if we'd lead the youth group. After all, our house had a pool and I co-owned a box at the sports complex. For the church's teens, there was the allure of tickets to the monster truck show. Don and I said yes. We were, I later learned, the very kind of family every faith group loves to welcome. The fact that I was going through a kind of prolonged panic attack didn't arise, but we were just so delighted to be welcomed at all.

I've often said that my main motivation in life has always been the man running behind me with an axe, by which I meant, survival. Now with children and a partner, others' survival mattered as well. Without my hefty income nothing worked financially. When the business started failing, I tried to keep it together, but it became increasingly impossible. When an enterprise you've poured years into fails, it's like a real death. Worse, it's like a death you caused, at least in part.

Church saved me. Being in the personnel field, I'd always said that if a job came across my desk that was better than running my own company, I'd go for it. No job ever had until I witnessed Ken doing his. His job was better. It paid terribly but it was clearly better. I loved reading and wrestling with scripture. I loved being a part of a community based on compassion. You didn't have to like everyone, but you did have to love them. I was nourished by the prayer and mystery and spirituality. Walking into a church, I didn't have to leave my brains at the door, as I had thought I would have to. My assumption about church, having been raised without it, was that I would need to give assent to propositions I simply didn't agree with or at least, didn't understand. The opposite was true. There was never any sense that doubt, disbelief, and inquiry were unwelcome, even to this day.

If we sold the big house and downsized, I could go back to school, to seminary. I'd have to keep some clients going, but it could work. Of course, it would mean going from wealth to just above the poverty line, but we could possibly make it work. Ordination wasn't the aim. I was just following my bliss, and I needed to stop the anxiety and the hideous financial pressure. In this respect, the recession of the early nineties was a blessing in disguise. I would never have been able to walk away from that much money without it. "It is easier for a camel to go through the eye of a needle than for a rich person to enter God's realm."

So that's what we did. We sold the big house and moved back downtown to a house that would have fit into our basement in the suburbs. The women who worked for me continued on their own with difficulty, and I returned to school. It was at seminary that I really could say I was becoming Christian. I remember the lecture where the professor, David Demson, who eventually became my doctoral dissertation supervisor, provided clarity. He was teaching about the reformers. He said something along the lines of, "For the Christian Reformation, Christ not the Church became critical. One understood 'God' through the Jesus of scripture, not the other way around. You aren't a 'deist' with a new prophet. You are a follower of Christ. Christ made manifest what deity means."

Now that made sense. Christianity had much more in common with the spiritualities of the Far East, with Buddhism, than with what I came to think of as "blob God" or "Lord" or "Omniscient Other." Jesus, as historical figure, healed, taught, talked. That was all I really needed to understand the Divine. Or, as another student said, "It is as if we are ants speaking about a human when we engage in God talk, but then a human came to us as an ant and we got it." Jesus was undoubtedly socialist. He was also the embodiment of Marx's true communist. In Acts, the disciples shared everything together. Early Christian communities mirrored the communes in Spain before the Spanish Civil War. The great Christian proclamation, "Christ has died, Christ is risen, Christ will come again," was the true opening to interfaith conversation. No one expected Jesus to come as he did the first time around. Christ could reappear at any time in the form of a Muslim, Jew (again), Hindu, Buddhist, etc. Who were we to control that? Loving one's neighbour meant absolutely everyone. Everything was coming together.

Meanwhile, on the home front, my marriage was coming apart. Don's drinking was spiralling out of control. I was not present in any meaningful way. I had a new "man with an axe"—the fear of everything falling apart again. We'd been together for seventeen years and were still best friends, but we'd both had relationships apart from our marriage over the years, and that was also destructive. We hadn't been able to make it work without hurting each other. The added financial pressures of the recession and the loss of my business were too much. We separated. My children learned trauma for the first time and missed their old lifestyle. Money was very tight. I felt as if I'd dragged them all unwillingly into my new version of "good," one they didn't share. I didn't know what to do and I just "KBO'd" it, as Winston Churchill put it: kept buggering on.

Then things got worse. There was a knock at the door at 2 a.m. Never a good sign. A young police officer stood there. "I'm sorry to have to inform you that your husband has been killed in a motorcycle accident." Don was returning from work and was way over the legal blood alcohol limit. He hit the brakes too hard at a police radar trap.

CHAPTER 8
SURVIVOR

That night and in the days afterward, the profound presence of both evil and grace were palpable. By that point in my life, all my grandparents, parents, stepfather, aunts and uncles, and one brother had died. AIDS had destroyed the lives of most gay men I knew—Michael, I'm sure, included. Street kids I knew had died or disappeared. Don's death, however, was different. I'd been on my own before. Now I was responsible for my children.

Francesca, now fourteen, heard the police at the door. We fell apart together. Damien, age nine, slept. I had the distinct sense that I must pray by his bedside until he awoke. He was so small and so in love with his dad. It is impossible to describe that night now, but suffice it to say, I kept watch. I felt the presence of the evil only death can unleash. That night I felt that I needed to pray to attempt to keep that evil away. I pleaded with God to protect these children, who now only had me left to protect them. I prayed for me, for strength. I prayed for Don's soul. We were, all of us, guilty, innocent, alone, together, loved, bereft, sad.

The church was there, as I hoped it would be. Even though we'd moved away from our suburban church and hadn't really become part of our downtown one, Ken's church, our church, showed up at the door with casseroles and love. Ken did too. They were our support. Don's parents were absent, I imagine doing their own healing, but absent from the children, which hurt. I think the three of us were a painful reminder that they'd had a son. It was easier for them to pretend we didn't exist. A couple of Don's and my friends helped plan the memorial. Ken preached.

Of course, there was a certain degree of ugly predictability to the funeral. I was so used to funerals where a stranger said words about someone they never knew, someone precious to me. But one of the reasons I went to church was so that our funerals wouldn't be like that. I was a survivor. Survivors think that way. Now there it was. Ken knew Don. I'd bought Don two bikes, a Harley Sportster and a Triumph. They were Don's pride. Ken told a story about asking Don if perhaps they could go riding together one day. Ken owned a Suzuki. Don told him, "Only if you stay way back and pretend we don't know each other." Everyone laughed. It was perfect. The service was perfect. This was what church was supposed to be.

I remember Damien looking at his reconstructed father in the casket. "That's not Dad," he insisted. Damien was so right. That wasn't his dad. He needed to see that Don was not only his body. That we are not only our bodies. Don's body was plastic-looking. It wasn't the body of the man we'd loved. Important.

The sense of evil dissipated. The cruel irony of being a child of trauma and now having children of trauma remained. What also remained was anger. I was angry at everything. Sometimes while driving I'd have to pull over because I was so angry. Angry at Don for being so stupid. Angry at me for not being a better partner. Angry at fate. He seemed to still be around, and not in a good way.

One of our new ministers, Joyce, helped. We would meet and pray together that Don find peace. We would pray for Don and with him, that he move on, and that we might move on. It seems macabre, strange, and sad unless you've lost someone violently. Her ministry was exactly what I needed. The anger seemed to lift. His presence muted. Joyce also ran a single mothers' group, which was a godsend too. Christ is in the helper and the help, there if we know where to look.

Francesca, being a teenager, found her own help. She had a broad network of friends and I hoped she was getting what she needed. Damien, however, was more obviously depressed and vocal about it. His school called me and told me he had threatened suicide. He was only nine and I was sure he had no idea how to kill himself, but I knew I needed to act. I took him to our children's hospital. We waited for hours before a psychiatric intern came to see us. He asked my nine-year-old, "How much out of 10 do you want to die?" Damien said "10." We were taken to a ward where the first thing we heard were screams coming from down the hall. Damien noticed *The Simpsons* on a TV and started watching it. A nurse appeared and told us he wasn't allowed to do that as he hadn't earned the privilege yet.

It sounds bizarre and it was. That was standard medical procedure, I suppose. All I wanted was for Damien to speak to someone. The nurse told me the psychologist would be in the next morning but that my nine-year-old would have to sleep in a glass room, remove his belt and be watched until then. The nurse seemed surprised when I said I wasn't going to leave him for a moment. "Then we'll watch you, too," she responded huffily. The screams down the hall continued. At that point my astute child said, "Mom, I don't want to kill myself anymore. Can we just go home and play video games?"

No kidding! I often think of what would have happened if I'd left him there. Nothing good. It was a real insight into the psychiatric establishment at that time. Had I left him, I have no doubt he would have been re-traumatized. I felt for those parents who believed in professionals and did leave children, thinking they were doing the right thing. When I was in university and did a practicum at our largest mental health facility, I saw the results of our collective abandonment of loved ones to the system. No thanks!

Instead, I found a Bereaved Family Group that was wonderful, where a loving therapist worked with the children and we parents had a group of our own. No abandoning children. No drugs. Just care.

Church was again our mainstay. Now I had no question that this holy community was a place I wanted to work, that Ministry was a vocation I felt called to pursue. It was the small village that would help me raise my children. The children weren't so sure. One Easter morning I woke them, forced them into the shower and then, Francesca still with wet hair, Damien dawdling a half-block back, hurried them the few blocks to church. That's when my darling daughter said, "Here's the picture, mom, the dysfunctional family goes to church."

She was correct, of course. Inside we would meet nothing but dysfunctional families. There were unhappy marriages, divorces, kids with issues, guilt, sadness, despair, addiction—in short, humanness. I knew. I taught Sunday School. Very little in the way of Bible stories got discussed. It was more dealing with kids who were acting out. One Sunday morning I decided we'd have a trial of a particular annoying boy who'd been pestering the girls. *Law and Order* was popular and everyone loved that idea, including the accused boy. I tried to get some values education in there. We talked "patriarchy." As I learned again, church was where you tried to learn to love everyone but that didn't mean you had to like them all. Mock trials became a mainstay of Sunday School, including but certainly not limited to the trial of Jesus. The kids loved it!

My own children acted out as well. They didn't, like their mother had as a kid, leave home. Quite the contrary, ours became the "cool" house where other kids came to escape their own homes. Our brand of dysfunction was somehow more palatable then their own families' dysfunctions. I never imposed curfews or anything like it. I didn't need to. When my daughter went to a high school prom, drank too much, and threw up on the vice-principal, I had to go to get her suspension overturned. It reminded me of the many times in my own brief high school experience when I'd sat in the same place. I remember feeling blessed she even wanted to be in school at all.

My children were always much better than I was. The older they got, the more fun they were. I loved and love teenagers. It's such an absolute blessing to have babies mature into friends. The constant parental fear for their safety and the overarching weight of responsibility lightens and gives way to a shared love of life. But we had still lost something profoundly important—another parent.

One poignant moment brought it all together for me. Francesca was out on one of her first real dates. She was sixteen. I had waited up for her and heard her voice outside. Looking out my bedroom window I saw her there with a young man. I couldn't look away, a parent's predictable faux pas. They were waltzing together under the streetlamp. He twirled her around and then they kissed. It was so achingly sweet. So beautiful. It was a moment. I was aware at once of witnessing something wonderful and of having absolutely no one to share it with. No adult in all the world loved her as I did.

I was very alone and very lucky. We three survived.

PART II

LIFE AFTER DEATH

CHAPTER 9
SOME OF THE WOMEN I'VE LOVED

Knowing I was queer was a pre-linguistic discovery. It was already part of me before I had an actual word for it. "Queer," a word that someone who is queer was finally allowed to use, was at last not considered a slur. It fit. Yet growing up queer didn't mean much. We were presented with choices, unlike our designation male/female, which we were never permitted to choose. The choices were heterosexual (normal), or lesbian or homosexual (abnormal). The boys chasing me called me a "dyke," a slur back then. I had no idea what they were saying, but that didn't mean I didn't already feel queer.

I always knew I was attracted to girls, but then again I was also attracted to boys. In some dreams I was male. In other dreams, female. In literature or in movies, I was as likely to see myself as hero or heroine. Whoever had the cooler role. When I came out to my dad as a lesbian it felt like a small lie. After all, I'd had more sex with men at that point, but there was no *bi-sexual*, no *queer* terminology to use. I hadn't read Kinsey. I was a kid! I certainly knew from experience I wasn't an effective monogamist. The sexual liberation of the time meant I didn't feel compelled to be, but then again there was certainly an unspoken assumption that straight sex and love for one person only was expected. Lots of homophobia was in the air.

Looking back from a distance, what seems so clear is that women were the true loves of my life. Still queer sexually, no doubt, but where lasting love resided and resides in my life, is with women. Love having very little to do with sex.

■

The first woman I remember falling in love with was in my acting class when I was about six years old. My mother had aspirations for me, this strange little girl that she'd birthed. Mom was actually the one interested in being a star—and she had the looks for it—but was relegated to hearth and home. I, on the other hand, could be her Eliza Doolittle, I could possibly achieve what she had not been allowed to do. Of course, the enterprise was doomed to failure. The few small parts she managed to secure for me on kids' shows, I hated. I hated having to smile. I hated the work of rehearsals. All the money went to her for more lessons, so that was of no benefit to me either. The only bright spot was "Marilyn Monroe."

That wasn't the girl's name, of course, but I thought of her as Marilyn because that's who she looked like. She was a teenager at the time and had bleached platinum hair. I'd never seen anyone with hair that colour. She wore sweater sets that seemed so cool to me. She thought I was the cutest little thing. I played along just to be close to her. I'd never been in love with anyone other than my parents and grandmother before. Marilyn was my first real crush. I found boys at school icky back then, whereas Marilyn was all curves and perfume. I have no idea what happened to her. Odds are it wasn't stardom, but I still remember her as if she were the greatest of all movie stars. I followed her wardrobe changes and her makeup. She was my idol and I her adoring little fan. Without a doubt she was my first grand passion. I dreamt of her. I copied her speech. I couldn't wait until I was in her presence again.

■

I had a few other girlfriends during my street days but my lover of note in the 1970s was Sandra. She's the one I'm pictured with at the first Pride photo taken on the Islands in 1971. She was beautiful, bright, and had a job we all envied. She was a sales clerk at a store for the haute bourgeois, Holt Renfrew. It didn't matter that we were all Marxists and activists, their stuff was off the chain! Sandra got a hefty discount. Consequently, she was the best-dressed woman I'd ever met.

Our nights were spent clubbing and the lesbian nightclubs (no such thing as bisexuals, remember) were wild. Always undercover and afraid of police raids, our clubs masqueraded as "Ladies' Baseball Leagues" or just had a door lookout that kept the fuzz out. Sandra stood out because the fashion was "clone." Clone for girls like us was flared jeans, tight shirts, short hair. Most looked like gay boys although gay boys were usually better dressed. Older lesbians were *dykes* or *femmes*. The dykes were profoundly butch and masculine. The femmes looked like drag queens. We younger, hipper queers made fun of their gender play, considering it gauche. We were so judgmental.

Sandra instead looked like a fashion model fresh from Carnaby Street and I, with my long dyed black hair, had reverted, post-Trotskyist, to my glitter garb. The relationship didn't last, but then, very few did. She taught me that I could be loved by a woman. Unlike with Marilyn, I didn't just have to love a woman. I knew I was wanted and desired by men, but Sandra taught me I could actually be loved as a partner, as a confidante, as a person. Our relationship never included sexual fidelity, and unlike with the men I knew, that didn't seem to matter.

■

None of us were faithful, really. It was an era when penicillin and the pill took all the fear from sex. Probably the only time in history that was the case. Wanda was my other seventies woman love. She was stunning. She had long black hair with a huge white streak, wore acid queen garb, and was an MDA dealer to boot. Wanda was truly a walking fantasy and she even had a car! That's how much money she was making. Hers was a smart little MGB from which she dispensed her drugs and drove us around.

The cops knew about Wanda and she told a story about how they'd broken into her apartment just minutes after she'd flushed her entire stash down the toilet. She saw them coming from her balcony. Beautiful and dangerous, a winning combination when you're young.

I already mentioned Wanda's breakdown. She was the only person I'd ever met who ended up committed to an asylum. It seemed unreal at the time, someone with such a healthy sense of humour and so smart. What was also notable was the bizarre practice of not visiting people in the bin, as we called it, or in "stir prison." I don't know why that was. As kids it was as if someone in an asylum just dropped off the earth no matter what they meant to us. Some folks visited, but they were the minority. Maybe we didn't want to admit that we too could be busted or "formed." We all were a breath away from the same fate. If we confronted it, the superstition went, we'd get sucked in quicker.

In a sense, although we had other partners, I was just beginning to see a future for the two of us together when her mental health intervened. It felt as if I'd lost her even though she was still alive. Not visiting or keeping in touch with Wanda was inexcusable. Who was the Cheri of that era? She seems arrogant and narcissistic. In softer moments, I can see how that Cheri just seemed post-traumatic.

■

I met Jodi toward the end of seminary decades later, after Don's death. I gave her a ride out to a retreat. She was and is one of my queer saints. She regaled me, the way former junkie street kids always seem to, with dire tales of her past. I didn't say much on that drive. You never knew which Christians you could trust with the truth back then. She trusted me in a way I'd learned to trust very, very few, if any. Remember, I needed to work. Jodi told me the story of her conversion despite the risk. She told me about how when a kid she'd met had OD'd, no one wanted to take the chance of taking him to an emergency ward because they'd all possibly be charged. Jodi said in that moment she knew there was something real about good and evil and that there was a Divine that demanded real action from her. She took the kid to the hospital and saved his life.

Jodi and I became friends. Few queer women were willing to out themselves at seminary. She was one of them. We were both members of the Affirm group struggling to make real the Church's promise of inclusion of queers. She didn't know my past and I wasn't entirely willing to share it. I was on the brink of ordination and knew that, even if the national Church thought I was OK, I still had to convince a local church, usually a rural local church, to take me on. Jodi wasn't interested in ordination. She was aiming at chaplaincy.

For one of our courses, a Field Education assignment, we decided we'd partner and try to start an alternative service at Jodi's church, in a large progressive downtown campus. The congregation was skeptical. We explained that we wanted to preside in jeans, have a rock band play, and poster around downtown. No such service existed back then and the "progressive" church thought it sounded too right-wing evangelical. Looking at us, two queer women, should have convinced them that wasn't the case but no matter, the meetings dragged on. It was only a year-long course and it took us six months to get the first service off the ground because they wouldn't give us the green light. Our posters showed a laughing Jesus, and we spent our nights at clubs trying to recruit bands who would play for nothing. We put in an impressive amount of work with no return. Jodi was pissed. "I've had it," she finally said, and she walked. I didn't blame her. Neither of us were sleeping much. We were both single parents. The project had become a nightmare.

Finally, and solo, I got the first and only few services off the ground. Predictably, the first night we had a healthy turnout which dwindled over time into just the followers of whatever band agreed to play. One of the dads I'd met in Bereaved Families, a Sufi musician, came and performed. Jodi and I, who had become lovers, spent an amusing night with him, a Persian Muslim, where Jodi demanded that if we were to take him seriously as a potential lover he would "have to accept Jesus Christ as his Lord and Saviour." Of course, we were joking. He wasn't so sure and left. We three remained friends. He returned to the next service and told us there was no God but Allah. True interfaith dialogue.

Jodi, still one of my dearest friends, went on to marry Caitlin and have two more children. I will always remember something she said during that period: "It's not the despair that gets you, it's the hope." Jodi continues to be the person I call with church stuff. She's still one of the most irreverent reverent people I know.

■

I met Babs, "the Rabbi," as she struggled up the stairs during a doctoral retreat. We were all sequestered at a Roman Catholic monastery for a few days of getting to know each other at the beginning of our post-graduate work. She was carrying a fan, bottles of wine, and two large pillows. Her words: "I've been to these places before!" Sure enough, the spartan quarters in the height of summer needed pillows, fans, and wine.

If we didn't know at that moment that we'd be best friends, I certainly knew it when we took turns recounting our stories and how we'd decided on doctoral work in the first place. I told mine and added a detail about the thing I missed most from my moneyed days—being able to afford Veuve Clicquot. Not one of the impoverished Christians got the joke. Babs did. I could hear her giggling softly. Veuve Clicquot, or the "Happy Widow," as we called it, became our calling card with each other. We always made sure we had a bottle present at any of our many celebrations. No matter how strapped either of us were, we always maintained that tradition. We both remember that moment fondly. It was the meeting of two kindred spirits or of two "aliens," as we joke. As Oscar Wilde said, "Give me the luxuries and I'll gladly do without the necessities."

Of course, Babs was queer. Even though she and her partner Robin couldn't be out at the time, she outed herself to me. Babs had been a nun in her former life and a lifelong Catholic educator, and she was finally able to be out and get married (it was my honour to perform that marriage) when she became a part of her union senior staff. The "Rabbi" designation came as she had much earlier almost converted to Judaism and officiated at Seder suppers at their house.

As students back then, all we knew was that we were sympatico. We spent the days together laughing amid the weepy storytelling and serious spirituality exuded by the far-too-pious group. Babs became, for all intents and purposes, our spiritual director at Emmanuel Howard Park United Church, my first Toronto charge, home of the evening service, where the first legalized same-sex marriage would be performed. She officiated at the retreats of "West End Riot Girls," our women's group.

The retreats she ran for our West End Riot Girls had nothing of the dreary piety of our first retreat experience together. Nights found us in our pajamas dancing and laughing. At one such retreat we were supposed to watch one of my favourite flicks, *Antonia's Line*, when the video messed up. Babs proceeded to narrate the entire movie, complete with different voices, to much further hilarity. Just one moment in many truly spiritual moments, that is, the small, joyful ones.

She's the one I know who always cooks her love. If there was ever a time in my own life that seemed weird, it was straightened out at Babs' over some deliciousness and, needless to say, Veuve. Like the matriarchs of my life, we were out of sync with the religious world but not in our queer world. We often spoke about how alien we felt. Babs could cut through the bullshit that often emerged in religious life because she'd lived it much, much longer than I had. Later, during the frequent storms in political life, Babs was there as well, reminding me always that the environment was insane, and we were perfectly fine. We were. The truly queer do that for each other.

We were sisters to one another, forged in the midst of much death. Far from resulting in depression, for us it was a reason to celebrate existence every chance we could. Yes, rage against the machine, but by God, dance to its music. Laugh at it. True resistance. In her presence, Jesus didn't weep. Jesus jived.

■

Christine and Cindy were both divine blessings to me. Chris came into our church an agnostic and left on her path to ordination. Cindy came in not as her real self and left as a woman on her way to ordination.

Chris reminded me of me. She and her partner had a blended family they were fighting for through the courts, followed by a pregnancy and beautiful daughter. Chris had been raised in a social justice household as well, and carried some trauma. That included, again like me, a successful business launch and the concomitant spiritual unease. Within months she and her husband became organizers of our youth group and mainstays of our church.

I had the privilege of baptizing Chris, marrying her and Mike, and baptizing her daughter, Tabitha. She was one of the growing edge of our church then and my church now, young secular searchers. Conventional mainstream wisdom says they would likely never be involved in a faith community. Like me, she was that rarity. After her own ordination, Chris went on to start a drop-in for queer youth in her own church. I felt like a proud mama!

Cindy had been in business and a teacher in the IT field. I remember well because she wore a suit. That was highly unusual in our laidback community. Again, throughout the long journey of transitioning, as she became her true self, we, a queer congregation, supported and loved her. Her new life was difficult and when she became the first openly trans ordinand, we all felt the Church should have celebrated more. They didn't. We did, though. We watched as she gained a pulpit and then another one, knowing the journey wasn't going to be easy. We prayed for her. When she comes back for a visit, we almost always get together. Cindy is the very proof of the Holy Spirit at work, of grace. As she ministers in a variety of centres, even rural ones, people prove they can be loving and accepting. Her courage and her strength are astounding. Her historic life is the historic conversion of Church by God.

◼

Toby walked into Emmanuel Howard Park United, my first Toronto church, for a free meal because she was barely housed, on social assistance, and couldn't always afford to feed herself. We had built our evening service around a free dinner. Toby hated everything the Church had stood for in her experience. She had come from a profoundly toxic religious background, as had and have so many. She'd always known she was queer and transgender, and in her estimation the Church condemned all that she was. And it had. That's how hungry she was when she came in.

She watched as we fumbled through an evening service without a pianist, singing "acapulco," as we called it. Our church couldn't afford to hire anyone. She listened to what I had to say and knew of our inclusivity, but it still took her months of sitting off to one side, refusing to engage. It took a while before she offered to play for us. When she did we discovered she was a profoundly gifted musician. She'd been a producer, studio musician, and played with a number of celebrities. That's when Toby also shared her story.

Growing up in an abusive family, Toby and her trans sister hit the streets and acquired a heroin addiction. Predictably, that didn't help. One night she was attacked by some other junkies and left for dead. That was her spiritual awakening, nothing churchy about it. She had technically died but was resuscitated. During that near-death moment, she understood that not only was she one with the universe, but that she should live as the woman she always knew herself to be. She got clean and stopped attempting suicide. She also left the music business and her former friends. Toby was diagnosed with PTSD. The diagnosis only helped a bit. When I met her, staying clean was still a struggle for her. Sometimes she said she needed something to "take the edge off," but in many other ways she seemed the most grounded person I'd met.

Within a matter of months, she became not only the pianist in the evening service but the Music Director for the whole church. Toby and others started a gospel choir that still sings together today. She was one of the queerest people I've ever met. Now we'd call her *non-binary* and use the pronoun *they*, but those terms weren't common back then. Dressed like a hippie, Toby presented as Indigenous (she was actually Ukrainian) and male. Never feeling the need to be girly, Toby wore women's clothing only now and then. Mostly Toby was fine with whatever pronoun people called her, usually male. It was Toby's secret and one that was only leaked to those she trusted. We loved her as she was.

We did a service once honouring our two favourite "guys," John the Apostle and John Coltrane the jazz artist. We called it "John Squared," and the select group of street folk, crazies and druggies were the only audience. It was a profound evening. Toby riffing on the piano along with recordings and me speaking about John's Jesus, mystical, exalted, non-binary.

Toby was also a part of our women's group, the West End Riot Girls, and attended our retreats. At one such retreat, Toby, when asked, "What would you eat at your last supper?" answered with "Cristal. I'd drink Cristal!" Toby was on welfare at the time and could barely afford a beer. No one there had ever had Cristal. We thought we were extravagant with Veuve Clicquot! We laughed. Toby had left behind a whole life we knew nothing of.

When Toby died of an accidental overdose, she was buried wearing a miniskirt under her trademark jeans, and Babs and Robin paid for a stained-glass window of Toby playing the piano. I said at the funeral that we were probably the only church in the world with a stained-glass window of a trans person, when someone yelled out, "What about Joan of Arc?" Indeed, what about Joan of Arc. With Toby we buried another non-binary saint.

■

It would be wrong not to mention Elaine, although she's never been part of any church of mine. But I want to mention her because when I ran for political office, my opponents waged a horrific smear campaign against me, citing my drug use. Hardly a secret, I preached about it as a story of hope. The same strategists passed anonymous tracts to Roman Catholic households on my sermons and my book. It inspired a TV commentator, John McGrath Sr. of the CBC, to describe it as the "worst smear campaign I've ever seen."

When I won, there was never a mention from the other party of an apology. Except for Elaine. She was the president of their local riding association and yet she invited me out for a beer and did what is rarely ever done in politics, apologized. She made it clear that the central party had dictated most of the content, but she took responsibility for her part in it. That not only closed an ugly chapter for me but was the only time until much later that anyone in my political career apologized to me for anything.

We became and still are friends, even travelled together. There are, in political life, those rare moments when principles win out over winning itself. Those moments are always paid for in terms of one's career, that's why. Elaine took a profound risk by telling the truth. There were others who displayed courage later, but she was the first.

She was brave and out about her own mental health struggles and life generally. Women tend to be. Like me, she doesn't sleep much and gets up at ridiculous hours. If she or I need someone to speak to at 3 a.m. or 5 a.m., we're pretty assured the other will already be up. Profoundly reliable and honest and still on the other side, politically, that's why I mention her here. It took a woman to show me humility can happen, even in the political life.

■

There's nothing particularly unusual about Joan—that's why I mention her. She represents to me a type of church woman and volunteer without whom no faith community could survive. Joan was the one shovelling the steps in winter, making sure coffee was on, keeping the church going with sweat and duct tape, if necessary. She was there long before I arrived at Emmanuel Howard Park and she will always be there, through numerous clergy. I suspect Joan will be there post-death. It's her church in every way.

For me and for us, she was always the one that truly loved the place. When all these strange new people started showing up and when we flouted the marriage laws, she supported the changes, even if she had concerns. Joan understood love was the only route for the survival of the place that had given her life, long before I arrived. Years later, when a public celebration of that first legalized marriage took place, Joan was there and others who'd been on our board back then. They, and she, were true heroes.

Years after I'd left that church, I'd drive by and still see Joan there, opening up, putzing in the garden, doing what she always did. Despite all the criticisms, craziness, tempests of religious life, Joan hung in. Truly, the real Minister of the place. She's not alone. I suspect every congregation of every faith in all the world have a saint like Joan.

■

There have been so many women I've loved and admired, some as lovers, most as friends. They are the ones who change the world and have changed my life. When male histories omit women, or give them a precursory mention in a dedication, they omit the truth.

This is the truth. There have always been women who were true artists, philosophers, scientists, theologians, history/herstory makers. Men have used our work, counsel, advice, support, and love, and transformed it into their "output." There were and are great women and they stand behind no one. They were pushed back there, sometimes lovingly, often not, by the men who took the credit.

CHAPTER 10
RURAL LIFE

My first settlement charge, as they were called, was in 1996. It was in Brucefield-Kippen, farm country, miles from even a small town. At that time in the United Church of Canada you couldn't be ordained without having a post in a church, and you had limited say in where that post was. You were sent where you were needed, and for most new ordinands that meant rural. In a sense I was lucky to be settled within 400 miles of my home. Many were sent much, much further away with all the ramifications of that for their families. At my new post, there were two churches, basically set in fields, one with a manse or clergy house next door. I remember the sense of dread as I drove the two and a half hours from my big city to take a look. The house, a creaky old Victorian with orange shag carpeting and wacky wallpaper, was so close to the church and so close to our Treasurer that it guaranteed no privacy.

The weather in snowbelt country was purported to be horrendous and proved to be. I immediately traded in my vintage Mercedes 450SL, worth much less, for a four-wheel-drive Pathfinder. Even still, I later found myself in a ditch and spinning out on black ice. The torrential rain often rendered windshield wipers useless. I made one winter drive in the rural landscape snow-blind. All I could see was white, with no indication of where the road ended and the fields began, no lights. Thank God for a car up ahead and the hope that they knew what they were doing.

I'd already postponed ordination for a year so that my daughter, in university at the time, and my son, going into high school, wouldn't be too unsettled. My son, after taking a look at the place, refused to come with me and organized his own alternative, staying with friends and attending school back home. It made sense. I was expected to stay two years.

The differences were stark from the beginning. I joked with them that I had as much in common with them as if I'd been dropped into an African tribe that spoke English. It was true. In just about every way, we were completely different. They'd never had a woman minister. They'd never had a woman minister with an Italian last name. In rural reality, towns were Catholic or Protestant. A woman with an Italian last name was suspect. The suspicion increased when I introduced communion by intinction and not the little shot glasses that set them apart from the Catholics. Needless to say, queer didn't come up. Why should it? Except to say at my interview when asked that I was in total agreement with United Church policy. They didn't expect anyone to say anything differently.

The kids in my youth group had never been close to a Black person or a Jew. We went on an urban plunge that introduced them to both, and also to street kids. One of my youth summed up the difference after the trip: "No one knows you in the city. At home everyone knows you!" Being known was a good thing in the country. Anonymity was a good thing in the city. I loved my anonymity. On the plus side our youth group grew exponentially. We had dances at the church, just like way back when! There was little else for them to do. Both bush parties and drinking and driving took lives. We local clergy offered rides, no questions asked. They were terrific kids. The queer ones, I learned, left home but came back for Christmas.

Attitudes around money were opposite from city dwellers', too. For their annual general meeting, both rural churches published their revenue, offerings given by the congregants. Nothing unusual about that, but the names and amounts were also listed. Again, no anonymity. If you were a member and you gave nothing, that's what was listed. No one seemed to object. I once asked my Bible study group why farmers worked so hard when they were sitting on so much land. "Why not sell most of it and retire? Buy a BMW and live in Florida!" The women in the group looked at each other as if they'd never heard of such a thing and answered, "Then what would we do?" True. We city folk had no clue, at least I didn't until then, about seeing work as a blessing.

While I was there, two senior members of the congregation went through a very public and messy separation. In the city, one or the other of them would have been long gone from that church. In the country, both kept attending every Sunday and appeared at board meetings together. I was astounded. I learned that when your families have been in the same place for generations, you learn to work out the most galling of differences. Another lesson for me. In fact, there were two families, a farm apart, that had in essence switched partners. Even they remained friends.

Of course, country people also knew who they were willing to trust. That meant that small group activities at the church that involved intimate sharing didn't work so well. Sharing was something you did around your kitchen table, not in public. Got it. Meetings were terse and direct and over fast. Motions were passed with little or no discussion, and then we got on to the important work—eating. Food is the currency of rural faith. Pork roasts and beef dinners are the fundraisers and every gathering involves food. Previously a vegetarian, I learned to eat meat again when the welcome party held for me was a barbecue. I figured my ministry could become all about what I ate, or I could just eat the steak. I ate the steak.

The country folk found me strange too. Humour brought us together. I started every sermon with a section called Heavenly Humour, composed of either a joke or a story based on our differences. One was about wildlife. Like most urbanites, I loved animals but didn't have much of a clue about them, other than dogs and cats. So, when I moved into the manse and a sparrow somehow got stuck in my bedroom, I freaked out. I tried opening all the windows, but it just flapped around the room. My treasurer lived next door, a fact I had originally expected might not necessarily be positive. That day it was. I asked for his help. I figured that he, being rural, would know exactly what to do. Surely he'd have some long-known way of coaxing birds out of houses. He certainly had an answer.

Picking up a tennis racket, he entered the bedroom of the manse, took one swipe at the sparrow, killed it, and removed the body. I was horrified. I felt like I'd hired a contract killer. My congregation found that story and others like it hilarious. They found me fun. Over the months, bats, rabbits, and more birds made their way into or under the manse. It wasn't easy for me, but I learned to deal. Then, at Christmas, a wonderful aspect of our differences around animals came together when I suggested that we have a living nativity in my garage. The processional could then lead into the church next door.

It was the most magical Christmas Eve ever. Farmers brought piglets and a donkey. We put on a real manger scene with our youth playing starring roles. By candlelight we witnessed the unfolding of what was originally, needless to say, a rural story, before gathering in the warmth of the church to sing hymns. The smells, animal noises, and chaos were lovely and made a lie of our renditions of a quiet birth. Holy, really. I arranged for a donkey to visit my city church charge later, but it wasn't the same. It's virtually impossible to recreate even partially in a city. The very best Christmas I ever spent was also at the manse when we were all snowed in one year. My remaining brother, Paul, whom I rarely saw, his family, our neighbouring clergy, and my children all spent the day and night mostly in our pajamas. That never happens in the city.

We, my rural congregation and I, came to love each other. I realized how wonderful they were and what a blessing the entire experience had been, even if I knew I was called to be a city kid in a city church. Our little congregation grew as much as it could, and we even started a drop-in program with a kinder gym for farm wives and their children so that they wouldn't be so isolated at home. Years later I received a photo of that once-small group that had now grown substantially. Smiling women and children gazed out at me, few that I recognized. What joy!

We clergy formed our own support group. Any of the professions where people move from place to place, like some police and medical staff, do the same. Folk who stayed less than thirty years were defined as "passing through." Our little clergy group met at the home of Chris and James, who started their own winery in the basement of their manse, calling it the Mary Mother of God Vintage. Going out to a bar would have been pretty well impossible without becoming fodder for gossip, not to mention the long drives, so we made a watering hole of the manse. We became fast and lifelong friends, Clergy tend to move often, as they had. I learned much from how they set up camp.

The community of faith took on a whole new dimension in the country. It was everything. If anonymity was sacrificed, the payoff was a real village raising real children and caring for real adults. The long-term care was the best I'd ever witnessed, as those who could not be looked after at home were cared for by neighbours and neighbours' children. No strangers there. Ministry demanded little other than turning up on Sunday and running a Bible study class and my moms' group, so it was possible to visit folk in hospital or other facilities almost daily. I learned to find my way around farms, too. Directions were indeed different—"Take the second lane after the red barn next to the Miller's spread"—but once I'd found one farm, I found the rest in relation to the one, and so on. Often, when I'd get there, I'd find someone in their underwear. No point in dressing as there were never any visitors without an invitation, unless they were kin. I found it flattering that for some I was in that category.

I remember once when my children were in town, there was a youth group dance scheduled at the church. When we walked into the gym, everyone turned to stare. They weren't being rude. It was just that having someone new was rare indeed. Needless to say, my kids weren't impressed. Later, when I was applying to city churches and a search team came out to witness a service, everyone immediately knew what was happening. They were friendly, of course, but sad to know my time with them was coming to an end. They knew city mice and country mice were different. They hoped but didn't really expect city mice would stay.

The inevitable "call" came from Emmanuel Howard Park United Church in the west end of downtown Toronto. I was to start at the end of July, after my requisite two country years. When I'd first arrived there, I longed for that moment. Now, I felt not only as if I'd betrayed my country family but truly thankful for all they'd taught me. I would really miss them. I'm still profoundly grateful I was sent there. My first settlement taught me about community. Community means being together despite severe disruptions, shame, and difference. Community means a true disrespect for the trappings that come with money. Community means a place where everyone has meaningful work. Community means raising your children as if they were everyone's children. Could I be "out" there? No, and I don't want to commit the sin of romanticizing rural life (something city folk like me do often). But I do want to say simply that not only were my fears allayed, but I understood why people live there and want to. I gained enormous respect for a completely different way of life and a wonderful one.

CHAPTER 11
BRIGHT LIGHTS, BIG CITY

E mmanuel Howard Park was in the west end of Toronto and, when we moved in, our area was still considered "ghetto." The main drag, West Queen West, was vacated at night for the most part, except for drug dealers and sex trade workers. The large former mansions around the church were now rooming houses or small apartment units. Parkdale was home to many ex-patients of what had been Queen Street Mental Health Centre. Yet, there were older members of the church, like Joan, who remembered when the then-mayor worshipped there, and the pews were filled with the well-heeled. Photos showed that at one point full-scale musicals with orchestra were staged by congregants!

On our street there was almost a New York City mix of people— pre-Giuliani. Down the street was a monastery, as well as houses filled with artists, film folk, junkies, and sex workers. The difference from New York was safety. Our area was safe. The sex workers, many of them trans, were friendly if sometimes stoned and intrusive. One Indigenous trans woman, Jenny, used to rest on our porch. She was well over six feet tall with heels on, and at first I was intimidated. Later she became part of our evening service and a part of our life. All she needed was a place to sit and a cup of tea.

Every night, because our rented house was "on the stroll," we'd see johns drive in loops around the block, many with baby seats in their cars.

At one point vigilante teams had tried to "clean up" the area by scaring away the johns. Luckily, that period was over. After all, as the vicinity gentrified, we were the interlopers. It was the sex workers' home.

I was told Emmanuel Howard Park United had two years' worth of money in the bank before we'd have to consider closing. Again, I was the first woman minister they'd had. As was the rural reality, desperate churches couldn't be picky and hold out for men. Not that they didn't generally seem to want me. One congregant called me their "Hail Cheri pass!" I'd managed to help the fortunes of the rural congregation, so perhaps I could help save one in the city.

In response I pulled out all the tricks I'd learned from church growth experts, mostly American. We started small groups, single moms' groups, Intro to Christianity nights, healing touch programs; we opened a decent nursery; and of course, we started the evening service. Its first iteration was a casual worship experience with a rock band that failed almost immediately. In fact, although attendance crept up slightly, all my initiatives together weren't enough to save us. After an unsuccessful advertised gig, one board member was prompted to say, "If Jesus Himself came back, we couldn't fill this place!"

Finally, we all kind of gave up and planned how we were going to spend the last few years of existence. Homelessness and poverty abounded next door, so why not just be Christian and offer a free dinner every Sunday night for those who needed to eat? The first few I paid for myself, and then we struck up a partnership with a food bank and food distribution service. We let our social service agencies know. People started arriving. One of them asked why we had a morning service but not a service for them. Good question. That's when we started a very different worship experience.

As already mentioned in Toby's story, it took us awhile to find accompaniment, so we sang the only hymn that everybody knew, and we sang it every Sunday: "Amazing Grace." Even with Toby's piano playing, most people didn't have appropriate glasses, or couldn't focus on or read the hymn book, so our singing was mostly call-and-response or a few old favourites.

People with mental health or addiction issues had problems sitting still, unless they were actually sleeping in the pews, which some did. There was George, dancing through services or moving around. Someone inevitably shouted out during prayers or the sermon. All my sermons became interactive. "You're all a bunch of hypocrites!" Neil shouted, high on crack. "That's no doubt true," I answered. People who had never been listened to wanted to speak. Often Sunday nights would be a time to hear testimonials. Those testimonials were most often stories of addiction, getting clean and then (no hesitation in saying the word in a church) "fucking up" again. Prayers were pleas for help.

Communion took place every week, due to popular demand, even after it was discovered we used grape juice and not real wine. The homeless population included a lot of immigrant backgrounds, many with Roman Catholic experience. We wanted church to feel like church to them. The first services were small enough to have communion in a circle around the altar. Later, lines formed. When I neglected to take up an offering (who had money?) I was again reminded by an evening service member that the offering was a necessary part of worship. Danny dropped handfuls of coins he collected busking, making him the church's most generous donor, in terms of percentage given. Danny was the only one, morning or evening service, who gave a biblical tithe, or 10 percent of one's take-home income.

Folk from the service helped serve food and clean up, and a few became regular volunteers in a way busy working people couldn't. In a relatively short time, as the evening service grew, those volunteers became part of the committee structure of the whole Church. Morning service folk, skeptical and even frightened at first, came to understand that just because someone was street-involved didn't mean they were dangerous. Security was important, though. We learned this after our sound system and numerous smaller items went missing. If the sanctuary wasn't in use, it needed to be locked, prompting Jim, an evening service member to say, "Only a thief could break in here now."

In reality, knowing who was in our neighbourhood helped security and certainly lessened fear. Fear for the morning service children was alleviated when we all began to learn each other's names. "Those people" you met on the streets were now Danny, or Jenny, or Jim.

Church fundraisers and dinners were open to members of both services and both came. In fact, most surprising of all, it was our evening service members that prompted growth in both attendance and offerings in the morning service. People saw and heard about what we were doing. They understood our dollars went to clothe and feed and provide services to real individuals from our area. I remember one child saying to their parent, "Dad, that's your sweater! Look, Jim's wearing it." Charity became the sharing of goods and wealth in a truly Christian and not patronizing way.

Long before we became known as a sanctuary for queers, way before the first same-sex marriage happened, our congregation had started to shift and grow simply because we were becoming more Christian. Evangelism, I discovered, wasn't just another term for marketing but was actually a movement initiated by the Divine in sending folk to us, if we were willing to include them, who then changed us. We were the objects, we church folk, of evangelism, not the subjects. It became the basis of my doctoral thesis and later resulted in *Que(e)rying Evangelism*, my Lambda Literary Award-winning book.

Of course, welcoming street folk was already a queer action. Many of them were LGBTQ2S. That's why they were on the street in the first place. They certainly weren't the ones our board had originally envisioned saving the church. We all learned a very biblical lesson. Inclusion can save you. Hospitality to those who need it most is a gift to the giver. In that respect, we, as much as they, were needy.

Trans folk were also sent to us by a Divine who cared about our welfare. It started with sex trade workers but, with the publicity we were getting, other trans folk arrived as well. The divide between morning and evening softened. Even our Sunday School was growing with the presence of young families in the morning service. Families liked what we stood for—"traditional" families as well as those who weren't "traditional," just like mine wasn't. Evening folk came to morning services sometimes. Morning folk came to evening services sometimes. Our social circles expanded in unexpected ways.

It all seemed to culminate in a Christmas Eve service. We'd invited a local gospel-bluegrass group to play and had candles lit. Toronto's largest radio station picked it up and broadcast an announcement for it. The sanctuary was packed with standing room only. That night was about a birth. It was profoundly emotional. To this day, Christmas Eve there finds the sanctuary full. Emmanuel Howard Park United, now Roncesvalles United, is still a vibrant church. It not only survived—it thrived because of Her, Ruach, the Holy Spirit.

The performance of the first legal same-sex marriage only helped that along. When Paula and Blanca asked me to marry them in 2001 and we decided to do it by reading the banns in the hopes of bypassing City Hall and perhaps getting an actual licence, I said "Yes!" My board backed me, but my reasoning was that if I didn't ask board approval for a heterosexual marriage, why should this one be any different? Too many clergy back then made it someone else's ethical issue and not their own. Like the Talmud says, "Who if not you? When if not now?"

Like everyone else who, queer or not, walked through our doors, I assumed Paula and Blanca were sent by God. That's what theology came to mean for us. There was nothing new in that. Love found a way and their licence arrived some time later. The passage I read at their ceremony, was classic Paul from 1 Corinthians 13, "...and now abide, faith, hope and love, these three, but the greatest of these is love." Love being *agape*, not *eros*. Agape, God's love, not eroticized human love, went through us in terms of justice making. Their marriage was an act of justice, and therefore love.

The ceremony was just them and two witnesses, a joyful, holy moment without expense or drama. When the licence arrived, a friend of theirs called the press and that's when all hell broke loose. Or was it heaven?

After the country's largest daily, the *Toronto Star*, reported it, and others followed suit, I was issued a letter from the Registrar General's office, a division of the Ontario Government that licenses marriages, stating that they were going to revoke my licence. This was an attempt to take away my ability to minister. I immediately appealed to my governing Church body for help. After all, hadn't the United Church been the brave institution and one of the first in the world to ordain openly gay and lesbian clergy? We had no doubt a response and statement would be forthcoming. This was history-making, and in a United Church at that!

Instead, there came no answer. We sent the request twice. Still, crickets. During that time, we received numerous threats, even attracting the attention of Fred Phelps and the Westboro Baptist Church—those Neanderthals who protest at gay funerals. They said, "The lesbian sodomite juggernaut rolls on in Toronto." It was funny enough that I suggested having T-shirts made, but it was also indicative of how under siege we were. We never heard anything from the United Church of Canada: no support, no encouragement, nothing. If I had left it up to them, I would have lost my licence.

Our situation was becoming unsafe. We were all frightened. Our most vulnerable evening service folk, our queer evening service congregants, were becoming particularly frightened. Our church wasn't feeling like a sanctuary anymore.

I called a lawyer, Doug Elliott, the same one who was making news fighting in the courts for equal marriage. I called our national media, the CBC. They were extremely supportive. We let them know how at risk we, and also the brides themselves, Paula and Blanca, were becoming. Doug sent a nasty letter to the registrar's office. The CBC covered the debacle. The registrar backed off. Years later I heard that the situation had been hotly debated at Queen's Park, our provincial legislature. When the registrar went silent, we breathed again and for the first time in months queers started finding us. We were becoming a sanctuary again.

Within a year, the Ontario Superior Court ruled that denying marriage to same-sex couples flew in the face of our Charter of Rights and Freedoms. The federal government came on side years later, in 2005. The marriage stood. We had won. Paula and Blanca and our entire brave congregation won. Church (The United Church of Canada) and state, with their perceived powers, had lost a battle with love. Profoundly biblical.

Paula and Blanca appeared on talk shows, especially Latino talk shows. We marched in our large Pride Parade and for many years were the only Church in the Dyke Day parade. I rented a convertible and they, in donated designer gowns, sat in the back and waved at adoring thousands. The Ontario Conservative Government was defeated, and it seemed, truly, that the Holy Spirit had graced us with Her power. We carried on, despite our denomination. For all intents and purposes, we were congregationalist. Who needed them?

It was around that time that my local Member of Parliament, Peggy Nash, asked if she could have lunch with me. She'd shown up to a service or two before that and I assumed that was the politically astute move on her part, since we had made news, good news. She was a member of the New Democratic Party, the social democratic party I'd tried to infiltrate as a Trotskyist so long ago. She knew I'd once been a member. I had no clue why she wanted to see me now.

I should have known. Political parties, whether on the left or right, want to win. They want candidates who can win. That means candidates who are known in their districts and can potentially keep seats or defeat incumbents. Little did I know that an entire committee had been formed, including some congregants, to do a candidate search, and my name had risen to the top. They thought I could win.

The seat in our area had been vacated by a high-ranking cabinet member in the provincial government who now was running for leadership of the Liberal Party of Canada, Gerard Kennedy. Gerard actually seemed like a politician to me. Fair hair, the right age, straight, privileged. It had never once occurred to me that I might be electable. Queer, former street kid me? Who knew that over the years I had morphed into someone vaguely respectable? Even though I was well known in my area and had a congregational base, I was so naïve I couldn't see that it made complete sense. So, Peggy Nash and I had lunch. She asked me to consider running for the now-vacant seat in a by-election.

What would this entail? I didn't have any money. "No worries," came the reply. I'd be provided with a campaign manager and a fundraising team for the nomination battle. Nomination battle? I hadn't thought about that. I answered that I'd have to consult with congregants. "Absolutely, do what you need to do," was the reply. I then met with my potential manager, Julius Deutsch, at Peggy's house. His ears perked up when I disclosed my Trotskyist past. Turned out, like many, he had a similar history. That was a comfort. I wouldn't have to hide being a socialist. Julius turned out to be the ultimate in campaign managers. I've seen his image in many political satires since. Julius was the high-strung Malcolm Tucker, the communications director from the British movie *In the Loop*. Julius was always hurrying and always clutching a wad of paper, the book he made notes in.

"That's the stupidest thing I've ever heard!" he'd say to me in such a way that I'd find it amusing rather than insulting. Julius, seemingly, could care less about politics or "policy wonks," always staying far away from all-candidates debates. Julius was in it to win it. His motivation was defeating the Liberals, the current incumbents. He'd convinced Peggy to run and she had won. Julius, like many NDPers, hated the Liberals way more than he hated the Conservatives. Without the Liberals we'd have a two-party system, like the Brits. We would be guaranteed more victories. His partner was a former Conservative strategist and the only person Julius would turn to for advice.

The enemy of our enemy, in our riding, was our friend. The Conservatives in Parkdale–High Park had no chance of winning. But their candidate helped peel away the right-wing of the Liberal party, thereby helping us. In one later election we joked with the Conservative riding president that if they didn't get their signs up faster, we'd have to divert our folk to do it for them! All of this was new to me, but I was a quick study. As a street kid and entrepreneur in my former lives, I certainly understood sales. I knew winning took non-stop work and a desperate sense of urgency. There was a man behind me with an axe again. Julius embodied a desperate sense of urgency. His justification was that, yes, you can effect change and make the lives of the marginalized better, but first you have to win. He'd worked in a former NDP government, one we on the left had seen as a huge sellout and failure. Julius had survived and landed in the union movement. He knew everyone and summed them up quickly for my benefit. "To know_____is not to like them!" The only ones NDPers disliked more than Liberals were other NDPers. Same as in every political party, I came to learn.

I was in awe and immediately, as most newbie candidates are, caught up in a whirlwind. I consulted with a few in my faith world who might give me good advice. Victor Hayes and Victor Willis—the two Victors as I came to call them, one a Liberal, one a socialist—provided the best political advice. Victor Hayes was the Liberal and admitted that they should have asked me to run for them. Victor Willis was the Executive Director of the Parkdale Activity and Recreation Centre, a full time drop-in and social services agency for our evening service members and many others.

Victor Hayes said, "Being asked to run for a political party is like being asked to the prom by the quarterback. It's flattering, but then you end up having to spend the evening with a football player!" Victor Willis offered, "I wouldn't wish that job [being an elected official] on my worst enemy, but I think you should go for it!" Brilliant, both.

Julius Deutsch and Michael Lewis came to the church service when I announced my intention to run and take a three-month leave of absence. Michael Lewis was a member of NDP royalty, the Lewis clan, whose dad, David Lewis, was once leader of the federal NDP, and whose brother, Stephen Lewis, was once leader of the provincial NDP. As Julius noted, "Two Jewish men go to church."

My poor congregation was crestfallen. That much was obvious. I expressed my own concerns in my sermon that day. The socialist left described the NDP in a mocking chant: "What do we want? Modest reforms. When do we want them? As soon as strategically realistic." Finally, though, I thought I might be able to do more for those crushed by the system in Parliament than in the pulpit.

Little did I know then that I'd find everything anyone had said about political life to be all too true, and then some.

CHAPTER 12
YOU ONLY THINK YOU WANT A REVOLUTION

First you have to win a nomination. Only then do you get to try and win an actual election. The nomination race, within the party, is often the most brutal because supposedly you're running against allies and friends. Nomination races are the foretaste of the truest statement ever made in politics, purportedly by Winston Churchill, Prime Minister of Great Britain. Churchill was speaking across the aisle to members of the opposition. When he returned to his seat, a disgruntled cabinet member said, "Why are you speaking to the enemy?" Churchill's caustic retort was, "I was speaking to the opposition, the enemy sits behind me."

First, I had to convince party members that I should even be considered for a nomination race. This took place in people's living rooms. I remember saying frequently, "I'm not a politician," but that taxes should be raised on the wealthy, nuclear plants should be shuttered, and locally we needed parks, not parking lots. The left of our riding association loved this. Julius wasn't so sure but didn't really care as long as they approved. "Just don't call yourself a socialist. It will scare voters." (It was okay to be one, just not okay say the word—not unlike being queer back then.)

The next step was selling memberships. The route to winning a nomination race is to sell memberships and then get all the new members to turn up and vote on nomination night. Like an election, it was a numbers game. It was sales of the most fundamental variety.

Later at Queen's Park, a young teenage arch-conservative, Sam Oosterhoff, defeated the President of the Conservative Party in his area. How? Not through connections, brilliance, or ideology, but through sales of memberships. I used him as an example later to those considering running, particularly young women. "It's like selling Girl Guide cookies. Same skill set," I'd say.

"Don't worry about the money. We can sort that out later," Julius said during the nomination race. He gave the job of collection to another volunteer. This went over well at the front doors in my district. Many of the constituents had little money. In most cases folk would happily sign up if they didn't have to pay anything, or at least not until much later. It wasn't much at any rate, something like $10 or $25. The actual amount we left to the collection folk. Did they ever collect? Maybe. Hopefully.

The reality of membership sales for nomination races is shady in all political parties. Occasionally it blows up into a scandal, but usually not until someone's opponents call it out. Problem is, if they know the ropes, your opponents are likely engaged in the same shady practice, so mostly no one cares. In my nomination race, both of us were signing up people with reckless abandon, playing to our friends and faith members, or further afield to those just trying to get you off their doorstep. Membership drives were often racially and ethnically tinged. I, obviously a Christian, signed up Christians. My opponent, a Muslim, signed up Muslims.

In another by-election, one of the candidates actually said, "Vote for me because I'm Chinese. Don't vote for him because he's Sikh." It was blatantly racist and it cost her the election, for good reason. The reality, though, is that political parties are ever mindful of the racial and religious make up of districts and prefer to run candidates who fit in with the dominant profile. Every political party does this. If there's good news, it's that at least some of the time the practice forces parties to run racially diverse candidates and the tactic can change the look of governments.

Going from door to door selling party memberships was the training for going from door to door asking for votes. The entire process was sales of the worst kind. Door-to-door or over the phone. No one said it directly, but it was whispered that I wasn't the party favourite. The other nomination NDP candidate's volunteers made sure I heard it. My team was too involved in shoring up my confidence to repeat it. Every political party has a favourite in a nomination race and it's usually very obvious. Even I, a greenhorn, picked that up quickly.

Julius arranged a meeting for me with the NDP provincial leader and with a few party pundits—all male, and all who made it clear they thought I was clueless. They were right. I was. Thing is, Julius knew this clueless, idealistic, socialist queer could win, and their candidate might not. The feminist in me just fought harder, knowing I was running against a man with official backing. In speeches I gave, I always mentioned that I was the first woman in my family to be considered a human person under law. We desperately needed more women in government. The nomination battle became gender-based.

On nomination night, a wealthy, gay broker friend ended up driving immigrant women and their children to vote in his new Mercedes. One of the kids threw up on the back seat. He then turned around to pick up some evening service folk who were stoned out of their minds. A truly unlikely merging of classes. It's not enough just to sell memberships; those new members have to turn up to vote on nomination night. In those days the way it worked was purely about the numbers. The NDP did not appoint candidates, although the party (like all parties) might discourage certain candidates and would often run uncontested nominations. It was an education for him. It was an education for me.

Once there, eligibility to vote is checked. Were they a member? Had they paid? Again, this process tests the ability of the candidate's team to make sure all was in order. A novice campaign manager can be easily outmaneuvered by a veteran at every step. Then the balloting begins anonymously and is counted with all candidates' representatives present. While that process happens, speeches keep the crowd from growing restless.

The high school gym where the meeting was held was outrageously hot. There was no air conditioning. The poor folk who'd been buggy whipped into attending had to sit through speech after speech by nominators, candidates, and the party leader, and then wait through two rounds of balloting. It took hours. Babies cried. Some of our seniors looked like they were ready to pass out. Most had worked all day. Julius ran back and forth, arguing with my opponent's management, carefully avoiding any of the speechmaking.

I had been door-knocking, walking and talking for weeks. Ever since my church had given me a three-month leave of absence, I had been working dawn to dusk. Even after canvassing, my kids and I were doing mailings, phone canvassing, and trying to feed ourselves. By the time it was announced that we had won the nomination, we were all so sweaty and exhausted that we didn't really much care. It didn't feel much like winning. It just guaranteed a chance to do it all over again. Many more weeks of walking, talking, knocking. We went home and slept.

Nomination races are supposed to excite supporters and get everyone ready to do battle with the real political opponents. The reality, however, is that the losers and their supporters often go home and stay home. So, the first people we had to win over were all of those disgruntled party members who now had to be dragooned into working on the campaign. The new members who had signed up and been dragged out to vote weren't really sure what exactly they'd joined. Nomination races swell a political party's numbers, only to lose a lot of the new supporters almost immediately afterwards, certainly by the time the renewal of fees come due.

My own church, which we were counting on for volunteers, was a case in point. Family, friends, colleagues—are all potential volunteers. Life completely shifts. But the congregation felt wounded and betrayed that I was abandoning them just as things were improving at Emmanuel Howard Park United. If I won the election, they'd lose me forever, so their motivation wasn't exactly stellar. Julius was accused of being a Svengali who'd wooed me away. Many congregants weren't NDP anyway and were tied to another party. This was all painfully obvious when I dropped in on a morning service and was cold-shouldered by people I considered friends. I understood the new reality. Even if I lost and came back, the church would be very, very different.

Never mind. The political battle had begun. My opponent from the Liberal Party was the city councillor. She had an unpopular decision or two to carry, but she had better name recognition than I had and an infrastructure we lacked. My entire riding association would fit in a small room, despite having won the federal seat. Diehard party folk who'd watched the NDP lose time and time again weren't enough to win it this time. All eyes in the province would be on us because this wasn't a general election. Julius and soon Jill Marzetti, my other amazing campaign manager, were rounding up all the support they could muster. The NDP had to back us now. The labour unions backed us. I was all they had.

I went from selling memberships door to door to selling myself to voters. I left the campaign office at 8 a.m., or earlier if there were transit stops involved. When the first signs went up, I think I had an out-of-body experience. All of a sudden, my face and name were everywhere. Media were covering the by-election in our riding because it was a kind of referendum on the incumbent Liberal Government's performance to date. After all, if I won, I would be replacing a cabinet member and a candidate for federal Liberal Party leadership. So there I was doing the jobs most people hate most, telemarketing and door to door sales, again. As with any low-level sales jobs, rejection happens more often than not.

A few moments stand out. On one outing, my co-canvasser and I were drenched in a downpour and found ourselves soaked, huddling at a constituent's door for shelter. We felt pathetic and hoped they wouldn't see us there. On another day, in crazy hot weather, we found ourselves lost in a cul-de-sac, dehydrated and almost faint, desperately ringing doors simply to ask for water. Every night after 9 p.m. we all met in the campaign office to debrief, get marching orders for the next day, and have a small pep rally. Sleep was difficult on days like that.

I was in a strange new world, canvassing at transit stops against my opponents, people I'd only ever seen on the news. Cabinet members were sent to our district to fight for their seat. Even the Premier of the province made an appearance. The process became familiar. Then it got very serious very quickly.

I'd seen the movies. I had heard politics was a dirty business, but then again so was drug dealing and even business itself. Because we were apparently doing way better than expected, the Government's campaign got nasty. They began what John McGrath Sr. called "the worst smear campaign I've ever seen!" It started with anonymous flyers dropped off at homes that might be Roman Catholic, quoting an article in which I'd been critical of the Roman Catholic Church. Of course, I had been! My entire ministry was based on my opinion that the Christian Right is neither Christian nor right where queer folk were concerned, and I didn't hide that fact. Those flyers had an impact with the conservative press. Then, of course, they went after me because of my drug and street past. Exactly what I preached about as a story of life after near-death to my congregation. We should have known they would. The message was always the same. You can beat this. Again, the information was anonymously sent to the press. Nothing like waking up to a mugshot of yourself in the paper with "Drug Dealer" in bold caps underneath.

This prompted my campaign to order that my Lambda-winning book be removed from bookstores, in case there was something objectionable in its pages and because of its queerness. The team were afraid of the backlash from the religious right. It seemed useless to say we'd never get their votes anyway. Every night and often during the day I'd be summoned to campaign headquarters for briefings held in the equivalent of closets, to be yelled at about the information being used against me. I explained I'd never hidden any of it. This was who I was—who I am. My campaign team called in a Catholic nun who'd endorsed me for the nomination race, in an attempt to change the message. I remember her saying, "Yes, it's been a terrible campaign on all sides." Clearly a Liberal, she wasn't going to help. I learned everyone is partisan no matter how much they pretend not to be. In this fight, God was one's party.

The effect of the campaign on those I cared for was what hurt me the most. I was in the midst of a nightmare anyway. My son, Damien, had to be kept away from the many all-candidate debates because he would sit glowering at my opponent. My children suffered. They had been working for me, and now they also were feeling attacked. I'd made the decision to run; they hadn't. For children that had already been traumatized by the violent death of their father, this was awful. I carried that guilt as I struggled on. My poor volunteers weathered it as well.

To say I wished I'd never signed on would be a significant understatement. Campaigning was a sort of relentless hell, and I was constantly waiting to see where the next blow would come from. One person told me they'd been offered thousands for "dirt" on me and would have come forward, but they didn't have anything new to add. At least they were honest. Someone else told me I'd likened Jesus to a serial killer. That would have been almost funny if I hadn't read it on a tract left at doors in my area. Meanwhile I'd burned through two pairs of shoes and lost almost twenty pounds. I prayed for it to end and crossed off every day on the calendar as if serving a prison sentence. I felt as if it was.

In the midst of the insanity I dropped in on the evening service supper at my old church just to clear my head and, quite frankly, to eat. One of our members, a street- and drug-involved man, asked me how the campaign was going. "It's absolute hell," I told him truthfully. "I'm counting the days until I lose and can just sleep again." His response shifted everything for me. You could say it was a moment of supreme grace. I have always found that the Divine sends me exactly the people I need when I need them, and here he was. He said, "Blessed are you when men shall revile you, and persecute you, and say all manner of evil against you...," quoting Matthew 5:11–13. Who knew he even knew scripture? I wasn't exactly suffering for Christ, but then maybe some good might come of it all. Maybe Christ could be found even in the midst of hell. Looking around that room that night, I was certainly called to put what privilege I had to use for those who had none.

Faith teaches that an angel will always intercede when you need one. Our evening service member's angelic presence coincided with another shift. It was as if the media and the voters said, "Enough!" Even some of the religious right came to my defense. Michael Coren, whom I'd debated on equal marriage and who disagreed with me on everything from abortion to queer rights, decried my opponent's tactics on his Christian syndicated television show (later, wisely, Michael shifted his opinions on LGBTQ2S issues entirely). The mainstream media dropped their coverage of the smear campaign and my campaign managers gave good counsel: "Don't engage. Don't give it air. Ignore questions about it and pivot to the main issues of the campaign." Political media training 101. Funny, though, I could barely remember what the real issues were. So much for my anti-nuclear, parks-not-parking lots, and more-money-for-education-and-healthcare policies. The issue had become the smear campaign against me and why it had no place in politics. In the end, it helped us win.

By the day of the actual election I was so stunned that my days had become a blur. The party assigned me an aide from Queen's Park, Kendra Coulter, who was extremely savvy. She drove me, coached me, and shepherded me, including buying me clothing when I spilled something on my suit jacket. She was the Whip's assistant at the Legislature and proved to be just what I needed in my traumatized state. There were rounds of media calls and more canvassing stops at voting stations, where it was difficult to ignore the near fisticuffs some of the volunteers engaged in—theirs and ours. I'd written the requisite two speeches. One if I won. One if I lost. I had no real idea of my chances. A first-time candidate in a high-profile political race, I had learned not to trust either good news or bad. Your campaign team wants you confident but not too confident. They want you hustling.

In the midst of the process, I felt profoundly vulnerable and frightened. I didn't really know what I wanted. I hoped to win, but if winning was a never-ending campaign, perhaps I didn't want to win?

We won. By the time I walked onto the stage of a packed hall, we knew we had won. Truly the win of the best in the business, Julius and Jill, and of countless volunteers and campaign staff. Turned out it had always been personal for Julius. Back in the day, he'd been a candidate and the smear against him was that he was queer. That explained a great deal.

It was a sweet victory in the sense that a negative campaign of the lowest order had lost, but the best part was seeing my children free at last, I hoped, from the nightmare. I prayed being a legislator was worth it. I hoped being a legislator was about more than just winning. I was partly right.

CHAPTER 13
THE BEAST'S BELLY

After the election win, I slept for the first time in what felt like months. I learned nothing political sleeps, though. The relentlessness had begun. Because I had won a by-election, there was no summer off, no "incoming class" of the newly elected. I was alone and I was to start work immediately. The Ontario NDP had only ten in our caucus, including me, a very small third party with no extra hands. The first few months at the Legislature felt something like getting my doctorate and starting a new business, all at once and within three months. I'd done both. I knew.

On my first day, I was ceremoniously walked into the Legislature by the NDP's Whip to standing applause. The same folk who had attacked my integrity only weeks before now were welcoming me. I had friends and family in the gallery and there I was, seated in one of those green leather chairs few get to inhabit. After the first session our caucus held a small celebration. A larger one came later in the riding association for all our volunteers. It was exciting. The only problem was that I had no clue what I was doing or supposed to do!

First things first. I had to rent a constituency office and hire staff. Hiring staff was a process and, because we had unionized staff, seniority was important. At the Legislature I was provided an office overlooking the parking lot—seniority again—but it was certainly the most luxurious space I'd ever inhabited. There was nothing in it, though, so another to-do was picking out furnishings from the great cache in the bowels of Queen's Park. Wandering through the storage area felt a little like visiting the valley of broken dreams. Members who had lost. Members who had died. Members who had left.

I also had to figure out what my role was. Kendra, the Whip's assistant, became my go-to person again. Until I asked my "maiden question" and made my "maiden speech," my role legislatively was to sit through question period and clap whenever one of our Members spoke, no matter what they said. I was to clap particularly loudly and stand if possible whenever the Leader spoke. I learned that because there were so few of us, I would have to shoulder many portfolios. I was given small business, employment standards, and housing, among others. Each of my portfolios was represented on the Government side by an entire ministry with dozens of staff and researchers. That's who I was to defeat in debate. The idea was to become an instant expert on all of the subjects, all by myself. If a Government bill was tabled on any of those issues, I would need to speak to it, for somewhere between twenty minutes and an hour.

Public speaking, for most folk, is the most terrifying activity next to dying. Add to that anxiety a list of topics you're shaky on at best, and try it in front of a hostile audience consisting of seasoned politicians. Yes, I'd had pulpit and Trotskyist experience, but those listening in church or at a Friday night forum didn't heckle much. To make it even weirder, throw in the fact that the Government can change the schedule without warning—and it's in their interest to do so. So one might spend all night making notes on one topic (and I often did) only to arrive at the "Leg" and find it was necessary to speak about something else entirely or not at all.

I also found out that the Legislative Library and its dedicated researchers, who are truly learned and experienced, would deliver you a doctoral thesis within a few weeks when really what you needed was a few pages of concise, profoundly partisan bullet points in about an hour. That's where the staff came in, but of course at the start I had none. Even after I hired people, I had little help initially since they turned out to be relatively inexperienced. I made my own notes. There always seemed to be either too much information or too little. I learned to do my own research, keep my own newspaper clippings, and write my own lines.

My poor staff spent almost all their time responding to emails and constituents who needed something. Thanks be to God that social media didn't exist when I was first elected! There were only dozens of calls and hundreds of emails from constituents, stakeholders, lobbyists, press, and others to respond to. I felt like I was being swallowed up, not knowing what issues were priorities and what weren't.

No one was to blame, really. We had so small a party presence that there was little help for anyone. I also learned, in line with the Churchill quote about where the "enemy" sits, that it wasn't necessarily in other caucus members' best interests to help anyway. I believe many were resentful of the publicity I was getting. In political life, if anyone's really honest, the quest for media attention is constant—unless you're avoiding them after a scandal. You need them. They need you, too. For both, it's a forced friendship.

Newly elected Members are alone until they're staffed, and once staffed, loyalty is the most important thing. The vast majority of my political staff have been like a second family. They were amazing and helped grant me the support and sanity the job itself constantly threatened to derail. Kudos to an astounding team for a decade, Carly Jones, Lisa Druchok, and Bhutila Karpoche, who eventually ran and won when I retired from politics. There were also many more interns, volunteers, and part-timers, all wonderful. Your team protects you, and a great deal of protection is needed.

We were all learning and always would be, but there were few real teachers to be found. I realized quickly that the next campaign starts the day after the last one ends. I needed to be everywhere all the time because my potential opponents would be if I wasn't. I needed to be at every store opening, organization anniversary, parade, market, celebration, funeral, business area meeting, charity kick-off, and foot race, and I had to host my own meet-and-greets, too. I was also expected to spend at least one day a week in the constituency office meeting with constituents. In Britain they call these hours "surgeries." I could never get a reasonable explanation for why, but no doubt sometimes those meetings were painful.

The painful meetings are not with consituents whose problems the staff can handily solve, nor are they the ones where a bill or motion might draw attention to a serious political issue. The difficult ones are with those you can see coming, where the constituent arrives with large binders, colour-coded inserts and briefcases full of paper. Inevitably their issues have something to do with a long saga of injustice, often genuine, at the hands of some bureaucracy or ministry. These situations are usually very real and very hopeless. Our standard responses would be along the lines of "You've learned there's very little justice in the justice system," or "You've learned there's very little housing in the housing system." It always put me in mind of a scene in Tolstoy's *Anna Karenina* where people sleep outside bureaucrats' doors waiting for a chance to be seen disdainfully for a minute or two.

Needless to say, government employees are also overworked and unable to change the systems in which they find themselves. We were all in this together. One ex-cabinet minister at the federal level described to me his main issue: immigration cases at the constituent level. They drove many of his staff to quit. One staffer had a complete breakdown. According to him, too many immigrants wanted in. Yes, he was in government, but there often wasn't much a government minister could do on individual cases; if you were in opposition, there was even less. Our main issue was housing. The government didn't put enough resources toward it and really didn't seem to care that there were tens of thousands on affordable housing lists. The answer is policy change. Welcome to Capitalism.

Telling people at street level with real-life problems that their only recourse is to foment revolution isn't the most helpful tactic either. No one wants to hear that. It certainly won't help get you re-elected. Now getting re-elected wasn't just the mandate of Jill and Julius, it was the focus in part at every caucus meeting, retreat, briefing, activity. While the electorate thinks that policy should be the point of politics, there's a term for those who focus on legislation: "policy wonks." It's derisive for a reason. I agreed with the electorate. "Only Governments can create policy. We need to be Government to do that." The problem is an old one of means and ends. In fact, if anything my history with activists and legislation proves, it is that even in a third party, with little power, one can make decisive changes that benefit those that need it most. All parties' priority is to want to be Government and stay Government however.

The sad reality is that when my party—or any party, really, with few exceptions—got into power, even with a majority government, they focused on the re-election potential of any policy. Hence, in Ontario, the Rae Government promised public auto insurance, then backed down because of industry pressure. Another sad reality is that when voters see that happen, they understand politicians can't be trusted to deliver what they promise, and often they throw them out anyway.

A majority government can do almost anything it wants, which is why it's such a betrayal when they don't. The NDP Government in Saskatchewan, with Tommy Douglas, brought in Medicare over a doctor's strike. It proved so popular it became Canadian policy. The Mike Harris Conservative Government, to every leftist's horror, did everything they said they would. Damn the thousands demonstrating on the front lawn of Queen's Park! Both governments were popular.

So many governments react instead of taking action. I witnessed a Liberal government in power for fourteen years that, with its dying breath under Kathleen Wynne, brought in reforms it should have enacted out of the gate. I've seen NDP governments, like Rachel Notley's in Alberta, get in bed with big oil and gas, for fear of losing union or voter support, and still lose an election. Unfortunately for us all, the right-wing ideologues are the ones that carry through on their promises to large corporations whereas progressive governments back track on their promises to the marginalized. When will socialist or social democratic parties finally figure out that multinationals are not their friends? Governments in European countries like Sweden, Germany, and Denmark had managed to bring in childcare, housing for most, free tuition and more, while still being capitalist! At the very least, we could do that.

What's needed is political backbone and principles. I would argue, even if you lose, you can fundamentally change the way government is done with a majority. Conservative and neo-liberal governments around the world have done just that. It takes policy changes. Yes!

Another very human realization is that those in political office —at least those I met —admitted they felt the same way too when they were being open and honest. All were frustrated by lack of real change in policy, real backbone, real principles over pragmatism. Independent of political party, they all felt the constant focus on winning was not what they signed up for. I witnessed so many Members who'd served, either in Government or in opposition, who felt they'd been elected to effect change and hadn't been able to. So many admitted, often over many glasses of wine, their diminished dreams. Never have I met a lazy politician or one just in it for the money. Most made more money outside of politics, interrupting careers that would be difficult or impossible to return to. Most worked more and longer hours than in any other profession I knew of. Our Blackberries and then iPhones saw to that.

If our political views were examined, most turned out to be genetic. Members' parents were Conservatives or Liberals or NDP or Green, etc. Some rebelled against their genetics but most carried on longstanding family traditions. I was one of them. I grew up in a house with a Conservative on one side of the dining room table (Ken) and an NDPer (Dad) on the other. The only thing they agreed on politically was that they both hated Liberals. Whether in homage to our parents or in rebellion against them, family made the difference. Not unlike other professions. As a pastor, I found myself listening to and ministering to folk from a range of ideologies—and liking them! We might never agree, but we were humans created by the Divine, after all. I would often remind my caucus mates that nobody really wanted a one-party state. In practice, of course, a one-party state was the goal of all political parties. They all wanted to be in power forever.

I often thought of my dad, long since dead, who would have been at the Legislature constantly. I was living out his dream. He could have imagined nothing more impressive than his daughter being elected to the Legislature as an NDP Member. I had an eerie sensation that this was a future he was somehow involved in still. One Conservative described how, when his dad, a Member in the Legislature, died in office, they had draped black fabric over his chair. That had an impact on him as a child. We all in some way had someone looking over our shoulders.

Once a Member in the Legislature, I had so many traditions to learn. Much like law, where there is statute and then common law, so every legislature has traditions and codified procedure. Each are volumes, and clerks exist for a reason. These black-gowned officiants are a Member's go-tos for procedural questions, and there are always procedural questions. Often the real basis of a question is how you might pull a fast one on your opponents. Hilariously, all of the tradition and all of the code can be overcome by a majority at least until challenged in the courts. That's how much power governments have.

Because of that, our little caucus was always frightened of being denied official party status if there weren't enough of us in the House. It was a real if somewhat extreme fear. So, I learned the limits of our so-called democracy. The real limits, ultimately, though, are what the citizens, the voters, will abide. Again, if winning is the aim, presenting as a dictator at the polls might not go over so well, but one never knows. I witnessed one such limit of democracy during the G20 meetings held in Toronto. While the House was in session, our government cabinet— in secret even from its own members—invoked an arcane law keeping people a prescribed number of metres back from public buildings. No one knew about the wartime provision and no one was able to debate or question its usage. Essentially, this law deprived the people of freedom of assembly, freedom to demonstrate, and freedom to even enter their own buildings, public buildings. None of us even knew it happened until it became apparent. Entirely in secret, civil liberties were curtailed with a predictable outcome. Demonstrators were herded up, imprisoned, beaten. The Canadian Civil Liberties Association weighed in, and some ten years later the courts ruled against the police, but the government emerged unscathed. The government was never really censured, and they were even re-elected.

Years later a Libertarian constituent came to me, irate. He said, "Our civil liberties were revoked and yet we had no ability to even know what was discussed and what decisions were made by the world leaders who congregated. How is this possible?" Good question. Even with all the researchers and clerks at our disposal, I never could find out an answer. As Emma Goldman, early twentieth century anarchist and writer, said, "If voting changed anything, they'd make it illegal." Sadly, that's even possible.

I learned every party has regular meetings at which key messages are inculcated into their members. The tactic with the press was to revert to those messages at every opportunity. Media 101 was the ability to pivot from the question the press actually asked you to the question you wanted to answer. Irony didn't work very well. Humour was frowned upon. A stoic demeanour was considered "statesmanlike," with the emphasis on *man*. Women had to refrain from emotion to be seen as serious. Whatever you did, you were cautioned against saying too much. Everyone in politics learned those lessons. On training for elected officials from American to British ones, the political messages to me were always the same in terms of dealing with the media. It's what makes most interviews with those in office as predictable as interviews with professional athletes, who also get the same training: "We'll just go out there and do our best!" The party line? "Our government is committed to the welfare of all of our citizens." Boring but safe.

As a newly elected member I was so out of my depth, in any case, that the last thing I wanted was more or any controversy. I was just trying to keep afloat in this brave new world, on no sleep. It was a world where anything could happen at any moment. Looking back, everything seemed so important at the time. The reality is that few citizens watch debates or legislatures in action, and a large majority of people only hear about the headlines, if that. In Ontario we were, in essence, a backwater jurisdiction in a backwater country, or so I was jokingly told over drinks at a conference in Missouri. We were not of global or even sometimes federal concern. After many years, I found it amazing if anyone ever commented on something I'd said in the Legislature. Yet all legislatures run on a mix of fear and self-importance, that every word said when we're on our hind legs is of note.

Every Member remembers the first time they rose to speak in debate or ask a question. Having spoken for a living prior to being elected helped me only marginally. My first question in the House was terrifying. After it was over, a grizzled old veteran, who seemed fearless, confided that the first time he rose in the House his legs were so shaky that he feared he might collapse. It's like that. Adrenalin keeps you going. Some members never veer from their script, prepared by their staff, for that reason. They simply read everything. Eventually I used point-form notes only, but never in question period. Questions are written for Members by the party, often central party staff. The stakes seem too high. Things like outbursts and storming out look spontaneous, but these moments are often carefully orchestrated for impact. As one Member said to me, "Under stress you never know what will come out of your mouth." I once said "crap and trade" on TV, instead of "cap and trade," and I wasn't particularly nervous that day.

One practice I adopted early on was to keep all press clippings about me in paper form. It may have seemed quaint to maintain my own archive, but digital information disappears quickly, and in politics history is constantly being rewritten. Not everything is Hansard. And even if it is on record, few take the time to look. I learned that lesson with the first legalized same-sex marriage I performed. Others were claiming to have performed the first legal marriage. The registrar book at the church was only part of the proof that we had accomplished history. The press clipping was the proof, including the photo of their licence. Later when the United Church of Canada attempted to deny they knew anything about it, I also had the letter the Government sent to the United Church Conference office, threatening my licence after the marriage was made legal (a letter the United Church denied receiving) and even the fax from which I'd sent it and re-sent it. The

United Church tried to deny they knew about the marriage but was proved wrong. Others to this day demand clarification about it. My archives, and in particular the acknowledgment by the press, were absolutely necessary in substantiating the historical fact. Those same archives proved invaluable in political life as well. When others wanted to take credit for bills I'd authored, I had the proof in the press. Women, keep all evidence!

Meanwhile, months passed before I was able to take any time off. My usual routine was to be at the Leg at 8 a.m. for a meeting, stay until 6 p.m. if not longer, and go home, where I did my reading and note making for the next day until past midnight or ran to some event in the riding. When the House wasn't in session and on weekends, events in the district kept me going from here to there. Time off, when I was able to finally take some, consisted of being semi-comatose in front of the television trying not to watch the news. Such was the life of the "lazy" politician.

Our little caucus really didn't have much in the way of discipline, which didn't help our cause of winning, but did give us a lot of freedom as Members. When I had an idea for my very first bill, I asked Howard Hampton, our then-leader, if I could table it and he said yes. That was the process. Still socialist, I wanted to do something under my "Employment Standards" portfolio, and a buzz was already in the air about our minimum wage being too low. It hadn't changed in years and was a paltry $8 an hour in 2006. I wanted to change that. I tabled a bill to raise the hourly wage of the worst-paid workers to $10 an hour. I thought it was the right thing to do. When Julius visited me in my new Legislature digs, his ears perked up. "Great idea!" he exclaimed. He saw this as my route to re-election and ran with it. What followed was an education in one way to make change happen, even in politics.

CHAPTER 14
WAGE AGAINST THE MACHINE

The typical process of bill-making, as I discovered, was to get the legislative lawyers to draw up a draft, read the bill out in the House and hold a press conference. With the $10 minimum wage bill, we had union activists and a few folk willing to come forward and speak about the nightmare of having to live on $8 an hour.

Many bills and motions are tabled by opposition members in legislatures across parliaments and republics around the world. A tiny minority ever pass into law. Despite that reality, most can still be used as organizing tools around an issue. Petitions can be signed and tabled. Stakeholders or lobbyists feel as if something is happening. And it sort of is. The press can get involved and become part of the push for change. But only if the Government can be dragged, pushed or harassed into action will it become law. Government Members can also table bills and theirs take precedence, obviously. Getting a private member's bill (that is, a bill not emanating from the government cabinet) passed helps re-election, so there's a natural propensity for any Government to pass their own bills (and their own private member's bills) and let opposition Members' bills fail. So for a third party with few members, getting one through is a battle with very slim odds.

Julius worked as an executive assistant in the Toronto and York Region Labour Council, which he convinced to take on the fight in the $10 minimum wage campaign. They got excited, too. It was a way for the union movement to prove they were pertinent to non-union workers, but also to support some of their own. We constructed a campaign. First, we had to get as many unions as possible to take up the fight and fund the campaign. Second, we needed their memberships, tens of thousands, to sign petitions, mount an email campaign (pre-social media) and hold town halls across the province. Third, we would make it an election issue. The NDP loved it, too. It gave all of us profile.

Politicians and their staff don't have time to read all the emails that come in, but the email campaign becomes a numbers game. It's a de facto poll, and polling dictates policy. Before social media really took off, emails influenced. Reading petitions constantly in the House necessitated a bureaucratic response and represented many real voters behind a particular issue. We needed to maximize both, and we did.

Meanwhile I was busy attending town halls and dispelling the myths generated by the right wing that raising the minimum wage would kill jobs and drive small businesses under. Neither had ever been true. Small business validators (those who already paid their employees $10 an hour) came out with us to town halls. Small business, the creator of 85 percent of new jobs, wasn't the culprit. Often, they had to pay more than the large chains because they couldn't offer the same benefits. We made it beneficial for them to display "We Pay $10 an Hour" signs (paid for by the NDP or the Labour Council) in their stores and offices. That helped them attract new customers.

I joked that I'd gone from working for one J.C. to another. John Cartwright was the head of the Toronto and York District Labour Council, our sponsor. He was well respected in the union movement and helped galvanize unions across the province as well as generate publicity across Canada. There was no doubt the campaign was a staggering success. For the women's march that year, the $10 minimum wage campaign dominated the banners and signs carried by almost every woman. It was a women's issue. Most minimum wage earners were women.

In the Leg, I asked nothing but minimum wage questions, as did our Leader in the House, and the Government was beginning to feel real pressure. However, their problem was with the large corporations that depended on armies of minimum wage earners to generate a profit. Those corporations weren't our donors. They were donors to the Conservatives and Liberals. Strategically, it put them both in a bind. Were Liberals really liberal? Were they the progressives they claimed to be? It might even tip the scales with voters.

Having a minimum wage above the poverty line is a profoundly moral issue. In fact, the minimum wage should be well above the poverty line in any community. I used Sweden as an example: with an 85 percent unionization rate, all their workers earned, in real value, well above the poverty line. Even their McDonald's workers were unionized. Sweden was proof that the large multinationals could pay a decent wage and still make huge profits. As an example of a social democracy, Sweden was a good comparator on a range of topics. Pharmacare: they had it. Childcare: they had that too. The Swedish model of corporation, government, and union negotiating everything from new roads to growth strategies actually made capitalism stronger. Who could object?

I don't think the right wing was ever really about saving capitalism or about fiscal responsibility, but that wasn't as clear then as it is now. It was only ever about making the rich richer. To do that, a weird pseudo-morality was invoked. Under my "Housing" portfolio, I asked the Government Housing Minister why we could find over $100 a night for shelter beds (all in) or hotel rooms for our homeless but not provide real housing for less. He couldn't dispute the numbers before him. He and I knew the reality: permanent housing, especially new builds, would take way more money upfront even though they would save money over time. The ugly political truth was that some other future administration might reap the political benefit from such a move. He was a Liberal. The Conservatives seemed to rely on the pseudo-morality that poor people deserved poverty and the wealthy deserved their wealth. Either way, the actual cost was higher than if we'd done the right thing and built housing for the homeless. Either way people would die on the streets every year. None of it had anything to do with saving tax dollars.

I used to joke with colleagues and friends that working in politics was like working in the Mafia. Every day was graft and corruption, and a good day was when no one got whacked. In response my bench mate, Peter Tabuns, told me of an instance when he'd been a city councillor of someone actually getting shot in an underground parking lot. Politics is also the profession where the higher you rise, the more you work, and the more difficult it becomes, until you reach the most powerful position, say President of the United States, and then someone shoots at you. A curmudgeonly old Tory who sat near me in the House also likened politics to the Mafia. "You can get in relatively easily, but you can never get out," he said. Also true.

Despite that, I was getting into a groove. I was surprisingly happy even while busy. Finally, all the *sturm und drang* of my political life was bearing fruit. The minimum wage campaign was certainly a success, but would it change the law? Would it change anyone's life? We continued to criss-cross districts and the emails kept coming. We knew Government Members were feeling the heat from their voters. In the midst of it, another by-election was called in one of Toronto's poorest communities. Immigrants, racialized folk, and blue-collar workers made up much of the area. It was another Government-held seat. Our candidate ran primarily on the $10 minimum wage bill and issue. That proved immensely popular at the door.

At the time my office had an American Republican student intern up from the Midwest. Though he was an arch-conservative, he proved to be one of our better canvassers. He was excited to learn not only about another ideology, party structure, and parliamentary system, but about a different kind of politics. I often wonder if the experience changed his mind at all. Being an intern and relying on my recommendation for his grade, he held his cards close to his chest when offering an opinion about anything political—including the minimum wage campaign, but he was a hard worker and definitely loved the Canadian door-to-door action. The campaigns he'd been a part of in the US were large and depended more on expensive ad buys and crowd organizing. My staff and I told him if he ever ran for office, we'd come down and work on his campaign. We said we'd hold our noses, but we'd put in the same effort he had for us. He hasn't called yet. I live in hope.

The electoral campaign was as brutal as usual, and our poor candidate knew he was going to have to run in a general election within the year. The good news was that he won the by-election, largely on the minimum wage issue. The bad news was that he lost in the general election and was historically the member with the shortest ever political career. But the wage issue had won and kept on winning. The major press was on our side too. Would the Government finally listen?

They did, almost. They brought in a graduated minimum wage increase over a few years, culminating in a $10 minimum wage. A small piece of pie now, they said to workers, and a bigger slice if you re-elect us again. Strategic thinking. For the working poor it meant a slight improvement on a brutal existence. So the $10-an-hour minimum wage happened well after the general election that took place within the year, although a small increase was offered almost immediately. Overall when you looked at median incomes across North America, they'd been more or less static since the 1970s. The rich were vastly richer. The poor just as poor. The middle class was disappearing as union jobs disappeared. The trick, ably performed by the right wing, was to convince the middle class, the voters, that it was the poor's fault, using statements like, "The immigrant is a threat to job security," or "those relying on welfare don't deserve it and should get back to work" (even when there are no jobs).

We'd helped turn the tide a tad. It was a victory for the NDP and for the left. The campaign proved you could take a bona fide social justice issue, build momentum around it, and force a majority government to change course. You didn't need a massive legislative presence. You needed to mobilize the grassroots and folk who normally don't get active. Our NDP caucus was tiny at only ten Members. The Liberals and Conservatives had almost twenty times our numbers in the House. But finally, it wasn't about us in the Leg. It was about those on the margins. The moment we won even a partial victory was a moment of grace for me in that, for the first time, I was convinced that I'd made the right decision in running for office.

What matters in a fight to change anything is the solidarity of many. The effort to increase the minimum wage was enormous, involving most of the union movement and their money. My bill was the legislative tool to rally around and focus the work of mass mobilization. The next decade's "Fight for 15" was even more massive and it, too, bore fruit, again not winning everything but winning something. The left often feel a defeatism about even working within the system at all, with parties or governments. There exists a "Revolution or nothing" mentality. This is unethical nonsense. Historically, all of the gains we've made have had someone on the inside as well as pressure from the outside. Whether it's women's rights, union rights, or human rights, gains are usually incremental but that incrementalism changes real lives dramatically. Progress is possible, even under capitalism. To simply wait for a socialist government would be a slap in the face to the working class who are assisted by those incremental victories. Working for a new world and a socialist government is in no way compromised by working within the political reality of capitalism. In fact, it helps it along, as the fight for a decent minimum wage showed. When we act in solidarity, we can and will win.

Our win on the minimum wage campaign also gave me my first taste of the patriarchy in politics. Afterwards, one of our veteran Members, a man, said to me, "It was very smart of the party leadership to put your face on that bill." I was shocked and responded too meekly. "No one 'put' my face on the bill. It was my idea and mine alone." He mumbled something like, "Oh, I hadn't realized." No apology for the obvious sexist overtones of the comment. Although it wasn't my first time experiencing political male dominance, it made clear that men ran the place. I'd been schooled. Our caucus meetings (and those of other parties) had a kind of bravado reminiscent at times of a men's locker room. The loudest voice often won an argument or silenced others, particularly the women.

Now that I'd learned how to work the system in which I found myself, I got busier. I also knew I couldn't expect to have the same resources or campaign built around every issue worth fighting for. There had to be some other way of needling, pushing, coaxing, or shaming the Government into doing the right thing. I would routinely ask Kendra, still my go-to person at Queen's Park, questions like, "How do I table a motion?" or "How can I stop a Government Bill at Committee?" She and Peter Kormos, my other mentor, knew all the avenues and tricks.

I described Peter Kormos as "the weird but ethical heart of our caucus." Peter had been a Member for over twenty years and was loved for his quick wit and staunch socialist credentials. He had been kicked out of cabinet for disagreeing with the NDP Premier during the nineties. Kormos was the only one who left the House, even though he was House Leader, when we voted transit workers back to work. In 2008, the Amalgamated Transit Union, the union of the Toronto Transit Commission, and the Canadian Union of Public Employees went on a legal strike, and all transit vehicles stopped running. I was newly elected at that point and bought our leadership's line that the workers wanted us to vote them back to work. I found out too late that that wasn't really true. It had been a popular political decision made within days of the strike action. Peter knew. At the time I asked him why he was walking out, and he told me, "I will never vote workers back to work." Principles over politics. He was also funny and a little zany. Another Member bought him a T-shirt that said, "Fuck you, you fucking fuck." That summed up Kormos perfectly. I inherited his office when he resigned and counted some eight half-empty vodka bottles he'd left behind plus years of newspapers. Peter died shortly after leaving office. The Legislature truly was his life.

Peter taught me that although the filibuster had been outlawed in the Legislature, you could still use a version of it in Committee to stop egregious Government private member's bills. I followed his advice on that score against a bill that would have made it legal for landlords to evict renters because of suspected drug use. Again, in an instance where even though the Government had a majority, we could be effective if we were armed with some knowledge. The bill was killed. Had the Government really been adamant about it, they could have prevailed, but it bought us enough time that the bill and the ugliness behind it was exposed, and it was dropped. A wealth of tricks are always available to members, who just need to avail themselves of mentors, clerks, researchers and others. I was inexperienced, but I knew I knew nothing. My willingness to acknowledge that served me well. I was always asking someone for help.

We were so undisciplined at the time that I'd often table bills or motions without asking anyone for permission. The ten of us were virtually free agents. It wasn't until much later, as we grew and so did the oversight, that I realized what fun that period had been. I didn't have to argue with a chief of staff or convince other Members of anything. Of course, it was no way to run anything, never mind a political party, but as a Member it was freedom. I tabled bills and motions on a range of issues brought to my attention by stakeholders or, just because in my own estimation, they were the right thing to do. At a conference on parliamentary procedure back then, I was asked why I was so prolific. I replied that tabling bills not only gave weight to stakeholders' concerns, but also sketched a full policy platform that I believed we as a party, and ultimately any government, should adopt.

Of course, the current Government never would. The bills would be a stretch for any political party to bring in, given voter opinions of that time. Over the years my motions and bills included building ten thousand new housing units a year, making housing a human right, automatically setting a minimum wage well above the poverty line, and requiring equity hiring practices, among many others. I held multiple press conferences with many different rights activists. In the process I was learning other lessons about the bravery of some individual Members and the hypocrisy of the process.

It's common knowledge that elected governments are wont to engage in the same chicanery their opponents did when they held office. History shows numerous examples of governments doing just that. When Conservative Mike Harris in Ontario cut education funding and set up a whole new funding formula based on per capita costs, the Liberals raged but they never changed the formula when they formed Government. When he cut long-term care funding and largely privatized the sector, the Liberals barely differed, all of which resulted in disaster when COVID-19 struck. Everyone also knows that newly elected governments break promises they made on the campaign trail. In fact, that's usually the first thing they do. In the election before I first ran, our Liberal Government had made so many promises during their campaign against the incumbent Conservatives that the NDP produced a poster detailing almost 200 promises broken within the first three years they held office, even before I'd been elected. We, the NDP, did the same when elected to govern in Ontario. As I mentioned, public auto insurance was one of them. The Conservatives in power now are busy breaking promises, as I write, from cutting jobs and funding to attacking Toronto's City Council. The sad result of all these broken promises is that voters trust no one. Yet parties will continue to campaign that way because it works. My political maturity came in realizing my party wasn't the perfect vehicle of change that it portrays itself as. My party wasn't somehow principled and ethical where the others were not. All politicians learn this, but will admit it only if they're honest.

I learned we were all wanting. That, however, is just the beginning of the journey. The aspiration after that realization is to do everything possible to make sure that what we publicly said was what we actually were and what we actually did. One can almost hear the too-pure left say that their party is different because everything would be perfect in a worker's state. As an example, it's far too glib to blame the horrors of Stalinism on poor historical timing or a power-mad individual. The Cuban revolution, although no doubt a leap forward from the dictatorship of Batista and worthy of support, still jailed queers and disallowed any freedom for their press. The far right says the same thing in pushing for their "no government" state or dictatorship of the few. One only needs to look at nineteenth-century capitalism, as free as it gets, to know the result was child labour and debtor prisons. Finally, ethically there is nothing more important than dissidence and resistance to any power that oppresses. Like many, I am convinced that capitalism is inherently exploitative and that economic equality, not to mention ecological justice, can only be achieved if capitalism goes. But even if the revolution happened tomorrow, the political duty would always be to speak truth to power. No matter who's in power.

As it is now, it feels too often as if polling dictates politics. Find out what we think the people want and then pretend to give it to them.

The sane approach is the theological one. We all fall short of who we should be, and so will all human institutions, but our calling is to change that, both from within and from the outside in. Not to adapt to it. Not to sell out. To tell the truth. It reminds me too of the old adage, "In theory everything is possible, in reality not so much." Or, as they say in legislatures around the world, "Perfect is the enemy of good." We need desperately to supplement that with "Yes, but perfect should always be our aim. Don't sell out."

CHAPTER 15

SHEROES

I had started in politics because a world of exploitation had to be resisted. I believed the struggle was more important than success. When all else seemed to fail, principles kept our struggle for the old goals of freedom and equality alive. I believed these words—*freedom, equality*—shouldn't sound quaint or idealistic, but genuine. Cynicism shouldn't be the fate of the elected. I believed in a life after death and a Divine I answered to, not anything or anyone else. I was a survivor. And even at Queen's Park, I learned I wasn't alone. Legions of individuals held fast to their principles and worked constantly to wring as much justice out of the imperfect systems we'd inherited, as possible. Most of them, in my experience, were women. Sheroes, I call them. The most effective lobbyists weren't the men either, or those paid to do the job, but the women who, while they didn't earn a cent, were passionate about their causes. I must mention a few of them here, although there were many over the years.

Fran Coughlin was not a political person, but she found herself on the wrong side of a stupid and cruel government action. Before I was elected, the Liberal Government passed breed-specific legislation aimed at pit bulls in 2005. It was a vote-pandering move with no basis in science. The Minister of Public Safety couldn't pick a pit bull out of a photo array of dogs, but I'm sure he knew this was a bill tailor-made to get press and promote hysteria. It didn't matter to the government that, at Committee, veterinary associations, humane societies, and animal behaviourists all testified against the bill. The Government felt it would be a vote enhancer. The owners of dogs affected by the ban held a rally and invited me to speak because they knew I was against it, as were both the Conservatives and the rest of the NDP. Fran was one of the main organizers of the rally and one of the first persons I met who was involved in the cause. The owners of dogs that fell under the legislation had already lost a court challenge and had no idea what to do next.

I told them that I would table a bill to overturn the legislation. Why wouldn't I? It came to be called Hershey's Bill after a therapy dog that happened to be a pit bull. By that point hundreds of dogs had been euthanized, the vast majority simply because of the way that they looked. As I said at the time, "This government legislation is so badly written that it would describe, not only thousands of dogs, but also all the men in the Legislature. Short hair, broad shoulders, strong bite and a long tail. We wouldn't know about the long tail because they all wear trousers." The statement was picked as CBC Radio's Queen's Park Quote of the Year.

Fran was the impetus. She never let up. She devoted herself to the cause because her dog, a beloved family member, met the description. Her "pit bull" was gentle and loving and had to wear a muzzle everywhere he went, and she, like other owners, lived in fear that someone would turn them in. Then she would have to prove that her dog wasn't a pit bull. Guilty until proved innocent. She, along with others, organized rallies, petitions, and visits to every MPP in search of co-sponsors for my bill. Years and years later, she's still organizing. Nothing about the issue was remotely partisan. We had one Liberal co-signer on one iteration of the bill. We had Conservatives. Fran facilitated all of it.

It's one of the lingering regrets from my twelve years in politics that I didn't get any traction on that bill, nor on any of my animal rights bills. In a stroke of cruel irony, when the Conservatives were later elected with a majority, Fran still had to lobby them to do the right thing, though they had always supported overturning the Liberal legislation and had even made it one of their campaign promises. As of this writing they still haven't overturned it. One of their members brought in yet another private member's bill to end the ban, but no action yet. I'm sure, however, that Fran will win. She will win because of her tenacity. It's personal and she won't give up. Multiply Fran by thousands of women around the world on thousands of issues, whatever the jurisdiction. These women are in it not for clients, or for money, but for love. These are the best lobbyists.

■

Susan Gapka is another woman who knew the law wasn't supporting her rights. As a trans woman, without status or money, she made it her mission to add "Gender Identity and Gender Expression" to the Ontario Human Rights Code (OHRC). For my part in it, I knew I wanted to memorialize Toby Dancer. Toby's death was an ever-painful reminder of the reality for trans folk in our world. I don't know if any minority suffered more than trans women and racialized, two-spirited trans women. Almost 50 percent of trans folk had attempted suicide, and those identifying as such had a 50 percent poverty rate. The Trans Bill to Amend the OHRC was one of the first I tabled. I called it "Toby's Law."

Susan had visited every elected Member, and few back then would give her time or take her seriously if they did. She had joined first the Liberal Party and then the NDP. Both had failed her in her pursuit of justice. She was never a Conservative, but she visited all of them, too. She'd been a street kid. We had that in common.

I drafted the bill using her words. There wasn't any hope of having it pass in the House at that time. If it became law, we would be the first juris-diction of any size to add trans rights to human rights. But governments are incredibly reticent when it comes to blazing trails. The Government House Leader and Attorney General Chris Bentley, not to mention the Premier, Dalton McGuinty, took the stand that it was unnecessary. They said trans rights were already covered. Their argument was challenged by one of their own—the head of the Human Rights Commission, a Liberal, Barbara Hall. She wrote in the *Toronto Star* that they should act and pass the bill. There was no political will. At that point, transgender people were seen by many as suffering from a mental illness. There were few trans con-stituents and way more right-wing religious. The Liberals, as usual, were frightened they'd lose their right flank to the Conservatives. The Liberals also remembered the religious conservatives who had fought them on equal marriage. Right-wing Christians, Muslims, Jews, Sikhs, and Hindus were all against trans rights, if not trans existence. That's who we were really up against. Much later, as the Liberals finally attempted to update the sex ed curriculum, the same voices were heard and seen in demonstrations outside on the front lawn. Never mind. With no one to say "no" to me, I tabled Toby's Law. The press didn't cover it. They didn't even care. The transphobia of the time was overwhelming. One NDP Member told me that if I kept standing up for "fringe" issues, I'd lose all credibility. Trans folk were not quite human in the eyes of the world. The change in popular consciousness since then has been astounding. When Toby's Law was first tabled, trans folk were seen as freaks, troubled, irrelevant. With that in mind, their rights were of course seen as unnecessary. The hatred, violence, and ignorance were substantial. That, I argued with people across the political spectrum, was exactly why we needed Toby's Law to become law. With the right-wing feminist (TERF, or trans-exclusionary radical feminist) backlash against women who weren't born that way (like J. K. Rowling's stand on Twitter), it's just as important today.

Susan kept on keeping on. She was persistent. When I speak about political influence at conferences or on panels, I never speak of paid lobbyists or policy folk; I talk about Susan. The last time I said she was the best lobbyist I'd ever witnessed, people laughed. They still don't get it. The Susans and the Frans of the world are the ones who change it. They act because they must. It's personal. I was honoured and privileged to assist them both.

■

As few are private member's bills that become law. Fewer still are brought forth by politicians who come out for stakeholders and issues purely on principle, even when their own party disagrees. No doubt, a good deal of debate happens around cabinet tables and in party caucuses, but making it public takes courage. We even have laws protecting the sanctity of such rooms—profoundly undemocratic laws, I would argue. These laws put parties ahead of the public. Speaking or voting against your own party is rare because it's usually political suicide. Loyalty is everything, as I've said before.

Voters and constituents find this strange and troubling, but these rules, written and unwritten, are a reality for the elected. My experience is that most people love someone who stands on principle and love when partisanship gives way to action. But speaking out against the party line is simply not tolerated within political life. When you hear a leader say,

"We're a big tent party with lots of divergent opinions," they're engaged in damage control. Threats from the party to the individual concerned have failed or haven't been used yet. Or that individual has given up any hope of a rise in political status within the party.

In that regard I have to cite another sheroe, Donna Cansfield, who at the time of this action was not only a Liberal but the Government Whip. The Whip's whole function is to whip members in to vote as leadership has decided. A myth circulated both at Queen's Park and at Westminster in England when I went there that the Whip had at one time actually used a whip on Members. The Government Whips do have actual whips, just in case, I suppose. The Whips would most certainly drag Members in from brothels and bars. Not so very different today, as Whips are constantly reminding Members to do management's bidding, particularly where the numbers count. That's their job. Parties will tell you that decisions are reached democratically within the caucus or cabinet room. Nonsense. Leaders meet with their management team before ever walking into those rooms. Leaders' and strategists' opinions almost always reign.

Like so much of women's bravery, Donna's actions went unnoticed and uncommented upon. No one in the press mentioned it. The media were rarely present for private member's debates anyway, since so few of those bills went anywhere. Thursday afternoons at the Legislature, the last day of the legislative week, typically saw the House virtually empty. Only Members who had to be there were there. The others had taken off home to their districts. I'm sure Donna's Liberal leaders were happy about that. If the press doesn't notice, it didn't really happen, did it?

The bill itself doesn't matter much. It had to do with oversight of the body responsible for children's welfare. It was an NDP private member's bill and a necessary and good one, but it had no chance of passing without Government support, which it certainly did not have. No one except a few stakeholders showed up, and they wore the same expressions as those who play the slots. Anything good happening would be a minor miracle. For that matter, even if the bill passed on the second reading, there was little to no chance it would become law. It would never be passed to Committee, or else it would be killed at Committee. After all, the bill dealt with an agency of the Government. Why would the Government vote on a bill amending something they controlled? They were happy, or so it would seem, with the status quo.

One might think that because so little was at stake in situations like these, acts of bravery, like speaking and voting against one's own party, would be frequent. Publicly every party indicates that votes on private member's business are free and not "whipped." That's a blatant lie. If they were free, it was simply theatrics or they had been vetted first. Members, after all, could always leave the House during the debate and not vote. Donna's act was unique.

As I've said, she was the Government Whip. Her leadership would never have given her leave to vote for an NDP bill that the Government refused to support. No chance. As well, she would be voting against her own Members, the very ones she was supposed to bring to heel! That day, however, Donna did something special. She spoke in favour of the bill and voted for it. Watching her stand in the House and speak passionately in favour was to witness a moment of real bravery. I can't think of another time when a Government Member took a stand for a bill aimed directly at her own Government's performance in its own Ministry. The Government Whip voted against her own Government.

Of course, it made no difference to the outcome. Just another of those women's acts of principle. The bill was and would be defeated. The only person it made a large difference to was Donna herself. She was clearly done with politics, or at least it seemed that way. She retired before the next election. I like to think that she, a woman of great faith who was active in her faith community, felt that she was simply going to do the right thing, this time for thousands of children. I spent some time as Whip for my own caucus, and if I'd ever tried such a stunt (as it would be described), I would have been fired as Whip immediately. The same fate usually awaits Whips of all parties. Being Whip means you're part of the leadership team and you make more money. There's little incentive to do what Donna did. Except one. She saw it as the right thing to do.

■

These are some of my sheroes. From active lobbyists to elected Members, I've witnessed lots of bravery over the years. Fran, Susan, and Donna are only a few of many women. Christine Elliott, a Conservative with whom I've disagreed on almost everything, still went to the mat for all of my LGBTQ2S bills. (Sadly, now that she's Deputy Premier, Christine voted to give accreditation to a homophobic, transphobic college.) Cathy Crowe, a street nurse and social activist, would always turn up for my housing and anti-poverty bills. Deena Ladd and Mary Gellatly, from Workers' Action Centre and Parkdale Community Legal Services, respectively, were always there to fight with me and others for justice. There were many, many others. This is just a sampling of an army of women who have shown they can be moved by principle and not just partisanship. There are still those who act without any expectation of reward.

CHAPTER 16
WHEN CHURCH AND STATE REPLY

Sir Walter Raleigh penned a profoundly cynical poem during one of his many imprisonments in the Elizabethan era. It includes this verse, which has always resonated with me:

> Say to the court, it glows
> And shines like rotten wood;
> Say to the Church, it shows
> What's good, and doth no good.
> If Church and Court reply,
> Then give them both the lie.

Who could blame him? He was, after all, ultimately beheaded by a combination of both church and court.

After much of my time in both church and state, I felt like I should have that verse tattooed. Despite the extraordinary individuals I'd met, most of them women, the overriding ethic of winning in politics and of fear in the church's bureaucracy meant, as it did in Raleigh's time, hypocrisy. How to work within such a system?

Within politics, we have so many examples of governments and parties attacking their opponents for behaving in a certain way, only to replicate the same behaviour. I remember an instance where both opposition parties attacked the governing Liberals for trying to persuade one of our federally elected NDP Members, Glenn Thibeault, to run for them provincially. The rumour was he had been promised a cabinet role. This sort of maneuver is against election laws, but election laws can be a bit of a farce since they're mostly unenforceable in any meaningful way. Parties are not supposed to lure candidates with promises of positions. If someone is duly elected with no obvious fraud at the balloting stage, however, bureaucrats are loath to override voters. Hence parties get the equivalent of slaps on the wrist for most infractions.

High-profile candidates in all parties have a good chance of winning districts and are often lured into running with some sort of promise. If the party attempts to deny it, *then give them all the lie*. So it was that when, predictably, Glenn Thibeault won for the "enemy" Liberals, the opposition called foul. Charges were laid. None of it really mattered anyway. His political career ended after one term. The Liberals were voted out of office, but not because of that. A short while later, I spoke to one of our backroom staff whose job was, in part, trying to recruit potential candidates and to offer them inducements. She reminded our Member making the accusations about the obvious hypocrisy, and he simply walked away. All parties have run smear campaigns against opponents. I learned that too. Again, if they deny this, *then give them all the lie*. When the Conservatives wanted to ditch their newly minted leader, Patrick Brown, it wasn't too difficult for them to look away or make sure that "dirt" was leaked to the press. It served a function.

The first year after my election I witnessed the Liberal Government send $32 million out the door with little oversight. One million dollars went to a cricket association. Despite the federal NDP position against pipelines, Notley's NDP provincial government backed one in Alberta. When anyone replies, *then give them all the lie*.

This is all part of a "means to an end" argument that the backrooms engage in. Most often, Members are not included. I once asked an MP with a senior role in our federal party about a decision they'd made that I disagreed with. The MP answered that they'd had nothing to do with that decision, but had to defend it after the fact. "But you're one of the most senior members of caucus. If you weren't in on the decision, who was?"

I blurted. They answered honestly, "Oh, some twenty-three-year-olds and the leader."

That notorious backroom really does exist. Advisors are brought in by management to poll, strategize, and scheme, all with winning as the goal. Senior staff are often tasked with this, and, if losing is the result, they understand they will also pay a price. Every party is convinced of its ultimate moral high ground and feels that the manipulative means will result in some halcyon end. The problem is that end is ever elusive, even for parties that win majorities often, whereas the means are always and ever present. At some point everyone in elected office has to ask themselves the question, "Is this hypocrisy worth it?" Sadly, I think most say yes. It's easier in opposition to maintain some integrity, but hypocrisy is still very real.

It's easier to be critical in opposition without having to prove you'd do anything differently—which is another sort of hypocrisy. The thing Members seem to forget, however, is they can only be fired by the voters, not by management. Management can make your life a living hell, but they can't fire you.

There's also the pressure of "What then?" As the saying goes, what hill are you willing to die on? My "hills" were to get the minimum wage bill and all the LGBTQ2S bills passed. To me, putting up with the hypocrisy was worth it for those who truly needed action. Hypocrisy, however, is the ocean in which we Members all swim. If I could find a way to get those laws changed or passed, I'd use all the parliamentary tricks, backroom negotiating, and press strategy I could. I knew my efforts might include losing status in the party, being accused of disloyalty, and everything that went along with internal party politics. It also meant going along with the hypocrisy if the cause was worth it. And if those "hills" would cost me my political career, so be it.

By the time I left politics after twelve years, I knew how to paddle along with the best of them. I knew, very much like life on the street, that people tend to act when they have very little choice. Governments and political parties don't want their shadowy sides exposed, and they don't like embarrassment. Finding the right moment to table a bill was a strong political tactic I learned. For example, most of my queer bills were passed when the Pride Parade was around the corner. The last thing the "queer-friendly" Liberal Government wanted to see was hundreds of marchers with signs saying, "Toby's Law: Trans Rights Are Human Rights."

There's an old saying, "If you're going to dine with the Devil, you'd better have a very long spoon." The maneuvering included timing the introduction of bills, getting the press involved if an important human rights bill wasn't going to be put forward, and as always bringing activist pressure to bear on the process. It all took a lot of work and my terrific team to carry it off. In that regard, politics, like most careers, involves, well, politics. Once you lose your idealism about partisanship, you can actually accomplish an amazing amount on behalf of the marginalized. As a socialist, I should have had no illusions about capitalist governments, and I only really harboured any when I was new. I tried to be upfront with stakeholders and let them know why I'd bring some bills forward for second reading and not others. I knew which bills had any hope of becoming law. With experience, I developed the ability to feel the mood and read the powers that be in terms of timing. I knew which cabinet members wanted to make names for themselves by supporting a bill, and when. Was it my business background or my street background that provided this insight? Who knows? Perhaps it was the same drive that had kept me alive throughout both. All I know for sure is that if someone of any party wanted to be seen as progressive, I was only too happy to assist in their quest.

Realizing that politics, like most pursuits, is profoundly patriarchal in both structure and makeup helped. Women work by negotiating. Men function by competing. We're conditioned that way. Understanding these tendencies helped in reading situations. From the frightening narcotics officers to bombastic politicians, I'd been dealing with men in a man's world for a long time. I recall one instance when I was the party's Whip that particularly illustrated the difference. During a minority government, every vote counted, and my job as Whip became more intense. On a Thursday afternoon when, as I mentioned, most members are back in their districts and only those who have to be there are, something unusual started to transpire. All of a sudden, Government Members began to trickle in. It wasn't even vote time. What was happening?

The male mode for management in my experience was competitive, aggressive. Don't trust anyone. Assume the other party will always lie to you. Return the favour. If you did bargain, it was to screw them before they could screw you. Better to walk away than to lose face. The opposition role was purely to make the government look bad, and that effort took precedence over getting anything done. This is played out all the time, everywhere, around the world. Though it may be astounding to many, there is an alternative.

So back to my own little goldfish pond, on that Thursday it was clear something was happening. I asked the Conservative Whip what he thought was going on. He was a hilarious man, who had once said getting arrested for a DUI in his riding would help him get re-elected. His answer was, "We don't know, but I assume they're going to table some bill or ram something through. They're probably going to catch us with no one here and call a vote." Remember, the real fear was with enough votes they could get just about anything done. Operating under that assumption, the Conservatives were already calling their Members in—they too started arriving.

I then went to the Government Whip and asked him the same question: "Why are you calling all your members in? What's happening?" This was something the Conservative Whip didn't think of doing. Or other men. After all, why would the Government Whip tell the truth? Who tells the truth in politics? The Government Whip saw himself as a feminist and a progressive. He liked to be seen as non-partisan, and I knew this. It's important to know Government Members at some personal level. That's how I could get bills moving on behalf of those who needed action. "We're not sure," he replied. "We think the Conservatives have some nasty bill they're trying to force a vote on and want to surprise us. So we need backup." Then I did a very vulnerable thing in politics: I told him the truth. "You're both scared of the same thing, and no one has anything planned. Just a silly rumour." Within minutes the Liberals left. They were followed soon after by the Conservatives. Everyone was relieved they could go home.

Acting out of fear and distrust gets so tiring. In truth, individual Members who had taken an average of seven years out of the most productive time in their careers felt stuck, and were. Those who came from law might have to start a whole new practice when they left politics. Those from other fields might feel they were too old or too partisan to go back. As one lobbyist described it, Members carried with them the "partisan stench." Great if their party was in government, but not so much if they weren't. Members, in short, are vulnerable. There is a real cost for entering public service, and Members don't take chances in an atmosphere like that. You were discouraged from fraternizing with your enemies. You could party with them, but God forbid you tell them the truth.

■

Toward the end of my political career, after I'd resigned as Whip and become Caucus Chair, I learned first-hand what it meant to be persona non grata. In my last election, in 2014, when I was still the Whip, I was one of only two NDPers left representing Toronto, federally or provincially. Our provincial election had gone terribly. Management ran a campaign on balanced budgets, veering to the centre, and then they did it again federally with even worse results. As had happened before, we allowed Liberals to outflank us on the left. It was a brutal slog of a campaign everywhere, but particularly in the progressive downtown core. I promised voters I'd take their message—what they thought of our leadership—back to leadership. It wasn't a positive one.

On election night, as I had done on every other, I had dinner with my "Rabbi"—my best friend, Babs. We went to a restaurant close to the location of the victory party that was to happen later. I asked my executive assistant at the time, Andrea Houston, who was also with us, to let me know the results when they were decisive. The last three elections I'd contended had been a relative skate. This election was not. It brought to mind another classic political line: "Worst-case scenario, you get re-elected." I wanted to win for my staff's sake, and for the sakes of those I was really working for, the marginalized, including queers. I had more I wanted to do, but I couldn't watch the poll-by-poll results. That's like getting eaten to death by guppies. My EA followed along on her iPhone with strict instructions not to say anything until we knew for sure. Once we had results, I'd leave the restaurant and walk across the street into the "victory" party. It was pretty clear it wasn't going well when I heard her puking in the ladies room, literally. Eventually we won by a mere 500 votes.

Almost immediately after the election, I kept a promise and invited Members who had lost and their staffs to a party at my place. There were a large number of depressed volunteers and Members, like Rosario Marchese and Michael Prue, who had both been in politics over twenty years and still lost. They needed solace and a few glasses of wine. The Party, overall, maintained the same number of seats we had, and added a few from 2011 due to by-elections, but losing the province's largest city was no victory. We had aimed to be, at the least, the Official Opposition. We had failed. Little was done for those who lost. In the fake Rah Rah, which is the official line on election night, hundreds were depressed in our rank and file, not to mention the Members, who had served for years. No one acknowledged what everybody knew to be true. We, as a party, had blown it. Our electorate knew it. The press knew it. Our opponents knew it. The Liberal Government was back and stronger than ever.

Keeping another of my doorstep promises I'd made during the campaign meant taking the message of our failure to our leadership team. It goes without saying, that's not what they wanted to hear. I resigned as Whip, becoming instead the Caucus Chair, an appointed position. It seemed a reasonable compromise. I didn't want to be a part of the leadership anymore. I didn't craft the campaign, but being part of management meant I would need to answer for it. People outside of the political bubble that is party politics often ask the same question I once asked: "Aren't you also responsible for the decision-making for campaigns?" The answer is, "Not really." The campaign messaging and strategy is invented by a handful—as my federal source once said, "The leader and a few twenty-three-year-olds." Members are asked for their input and then given the four or five key promises that are all worked out elsewhere. That's it.

I suffered for all our volunteers who, in that campaign and the subsequent federal campaign, felt like the party's failures were their personal failures. All the thousands who lived on the phone, or walked miles to knock on countless doors, or endlessly entered data—those folks hadn't failed. The party had failed them. Not to mention all the voters who felt they couldn't support a centrist campaign in good conscience. Many just stayed home. They told me the campaign stunk, and they told me they'd only vote for me if I took that message back. "Do better" was the message. I felt responsible, and if I was going to maintain any integrity or face anyone in my riding again, I needed to act. No one in the party wanted to hear it.

I didn't need to seek the press out; they found me. When they asked the direct question, I simply told the truth. I agreed to an interview with someone I trusted, Desmond Cole, a terrific journalist who wasn't afraid to tell the truth. Desmond later became a cause célèbre in his own right as a Black activist and author. At the time, he was working for a small publication, the *Torontoist*, but that didn't matter. The news exploded to the mainstream press. The leader called me on the carpet. She'd had complaints from members about me, and I'd have to answer to them at the next caucus meeting. Looking back now, it seems amazing that all I said was that running to the centre cost us the election! I said we should return to our socialist roots. I wasn't naïve about it. Even while I was keeping a promise to my electorate and quite frankly to integrity, I knew my statements would cost me, and they did.

Most members of most parties suffer through caucus meetings. They're a mix of pep rally, arguments, and, ultimately, marching orders, and this one promised to be especially awful. It was. My staff did everything but anoint my body before I left for it. I knew one thing for sure: they couldn't fire me. Only the electorate could do that. It was cold comfort, though. I awaited my fate.

It didn't take long. Almost immediately after I called the meeting to order, the others started in on how I'd betrayed them, how I'd betrayed the party. How could I say such things? And so on. One after another ruminated on my treason and what it would result in. I said nothing, simply acknowledging the next speaker on the agenda. What was there to say? It was more than twenty people against one. The meeting seemed to go on forever, but was actually only two hours. Mercifully, a few said nothing, and one actually came to my defense—the other Toronto Member, my former bench mate Peter Tabuns. What a mensch! He knew and had lived the truth of that campaign. At the end I said that I would be happy to meet with any Member one on one. Only one took me up on that.

That sort of abuse is like swimming upstream. Leaving the caucus room that day I was shaking, part crying, part laughing. It was no surprise, really. I was hardly the first to have done something like this, nor will I be the last. My prayers go out to anyone who finds themselves in that position. It grew so abusive and unfair that it almost passed over into something darkly funny. The path forward was clear. I was hated. They let me know that. Predictably, all the orchestrators of that campaign were quietly let go later, and the incoming Chief of Staff described our campaign as one of the worst he'd seen in some time. But that hypocrisy was later. For the time being, I had been disloyal. I was not a team player. Got it. I was summarily fired as Caucus Chair (although on paper they simply "changed the rules" to make the position an elected one, knowing that no one would vote for me). Their problem was that since I'd told the uncomfortable truth to the press —even a truth leadership ultimately agreed with—I might (and in fact did) do it again. They made sure I got a Committee Chair role, however, otherwise I would have taken a hit on my paycheck. And they were smart enough to know I would not "go gentle into that good night," as Dylan Thomas would say.

That's when I learned another key political lesson: the Richard Nixon policy called MAD, mutually assured destruction. Named after the stand-off with the Soviet Union during the cold war over nuclear weapons, it is applicable to understanding many political actions. Only the electorate can actually fire you, so even if a party boots you out of caucus, you still sit in the House as an independent. Your presence becomes that of avenging spirit. Not only that, but if they kick you out, the party loses the subsidies they get for you as a Member. Worst-case scenario, they might even lose your seat if you cross the floor or simply quit.

The price paid by the dissenting member is very high, however. It's like going back to high school to be the picked-on kid with no friends. It's the end of your rise in the party and perhaps the end of your political career. I still had some friends, though, and I had my staff. Because I was now cast as unpredictable, traitorous, and dangerous, the party gave me a wide berth. I was once again the "dyke" who outran the bullies on her way home and still called them names the next day. I wasn't sleeping. Now I found myself vomiting most mornings as I arrived at Queen's Park.

The party, as said, knew the gaffes of their campaign had cost them. They ran a very different campaign the next time around—part timing, part strategic shift—and became the Official Opposition. I truly believe voters want and need the truth from their politicians. They want apologies when apologies are due. They also prefer their own local representatives to represent them on issues and not be party hacks. Most admire a straight shooter even if they disagree with the person. I know I do. The irony is that parties who just want to win would win more if they allowed honesty and were honest themselves.

It got worse for me before it got better; that part is forgotten in the heat of the next news cycle. One day I was literally screamed at across a crowded cafeteria in the basement, in the presence of all sort of visitors, party folk of all stripes and employees. One of our bully boy Members yelled accusations and invectives in a public space. Mostly, I just avoided my own party and surrounded myself with people who wouldn't be abusive and with my own brave staff. My new policy was to record all conversations with leadership and to take my EA with me if at all possible. As a friend said, I'd have the basis for a lawsuit or charges but only if it became physical or sexual. Emotional assault doesn't count. There was no point really. I'd already made up my mind that I wouldn't run again. Over time, the vomiting stopped. I sought counselling and took antidepressants for a bit. If anything, the whole experience added fuel to my determination to use my time left in politics to do whatever I could for those who needed it. That would be my legacy, and my true revenge.

PART III

THE TRACES NOT LEFT BEHIND

CHAPTER 17

THE LETTER ALWAYS ARRIVES

In psychoanalysis and psychotherapy more generally, there is always an understanding that the "stuff" of our formative years, particularly trauma of any variety, doesn't just disappear but leaves marks, and combines with the demands put upon us by the world. Those traces affect our actions, our lives, often without us being aware. In a sense, the letter mailed from the past will always be delivered. It always arrives when and where it should. The debt always exists, until we pay it, and the letter sits until we read it. PTSD survivors understand that their trauma will come back again and again. If we want to survive, our choice is to respond in a way denied us at the time. When that "letter" from our past arrives in our lives, in our work, we can open it, read it, and act, or not. To me, there's nothing particularly heroic in learning this and acting. It's how we must go on, ethically speaking. It's what makes life worth living.

It took me decades to figure out that I didn't really grow up in a loving home. With the exception of my grandmother, I grew up in a violent, neurotic, narcissistic household where victims of their own past personal traumas acted out in nasty, aggressive ways. This is not to blame any of them. What good would that do? They're all long dead and gone. Rather, it's about learning to love the little girl that I was. The little queer, frightened, confused, often lost kid. So there's really nothing I have ever done in the political, religious, street, or queer world that isn't an effort to rescue that little girl and others like her. Mostly it's a debt to be paid up for all the times I hadn't.

A story from my young adult years helps illustrate this. Looking at myself as an early twenty-something, I'm now so aware of how lost I was. As I've said, one of my regrets from my political years was how little I was able to accomplish for animal rights. Well, that twenty-something Cheri had a dog, one I still miss. Sebastian was a Cairn Terrier mix and a rescue from the Humane Society. There is no way I should have been entrusted with a dog at that point in my life. As a result, Sebastian was left to wander the streets of Toronto. Oh, I fed and loved him, but I was still kind of a street kid myself. I was living communally at the time and was politically active, but I was still barely capable of looking after even myself. All of that is no excuse. When I think of how little I took care of this sentient being entrusted to me, I can't believe I'm that same person. Am I? I opened the door every day and Sebastian wandered out and at the end of the day, he returned—or didn't, forcing me to pick him up from the Humane Society again. It seems a miracle he lived to be fourteen. By the time of his death I'd become a parent, changed my life, learned how to look after others, but really never re-thought the actions of the younger me. Perhaps my animal activism is my way of repaying the debt. In that sense, it's certainly owed. Nothing particularly laudable about it.

All my queer rights bills, the sleepless nights, the health consequences of fighting with every and any authority to get something done—aren't these actions also simply a way of repaying the debt left to me for that little lost girl from Bedford Road? I know damn well that as I write, children are being bullied, chased, threatened, and even killed because they're queer. No one can save them all, but maybe we can save one. Maybe I can help her, some new little Cheri. I'm not one for false modesty. The fact is that the legacy is simply doing what is needed. All survivors will understand that "making amends" is essential to our own health. It's not exceptional. More like taking necessary medication. I need to do it.

The consumerist world we all live in sells us the idea that simply by gratifying hedonistic desires, making more money and spending more money, we'll be happy. Anyone who enters the public sphere probably gets that there's no real happiness out there. In a wry twist, the best thing you can do to help yourself is to help others. It sounds clichéd but there is such an act. Whether we see humans as inherently selfish, inherently benevolent, or completely blank slates, acting for others is the only reason to live. For survivors of trauma, it's the only way we can live.

Like others, I still self-sabotage, act out of insecurity or resentment. I see myself more as a failure for what I lack than a success for what I've done. I'm human. In spite of yourself, however, you can make waves. You can "get shit done"! Where women act— in particular, trans, Black, non-white, Indigenous women—we have to act *as if* we have power or can get our hands on it. We have to act *as if* we were and are worthy of power. This, despite all of our conditioning and training, despite the huge cultural white, straight, male, capitalist machine that tells us we can't. Just do the impossible.

All of the laws I managed to get enacted, I did from a position of powerful-weakness. I didn't have any real power, but I did it anyway. As I write, we are witnessing an uprising of the Black Lives Matter movement, which has managed in a few weeks to effect change that hasn't happened in decades. Thankfully, this is an uprising that won't be satisfied until the system of white supremacy and the state itself are fundamentally revolutionized. This is some powerful-weakness! They, *we*, don't have the guns or the money, but we have the will and the voices and the desire for a new world. Just do the impossible.

Every revolution seemed impossible until it happened. My advice is not to wait. Make things happen. Use everything that's been given to you, all the trauma, all the suffering, all the crap, and forge it into a weapon of your own and others' redemption. Don't hold back. As I used to say to all the ethical activists, "There's no question you will win. The only question is *when?*" Just do the impossible.

CHAPTER 18

HOW TO GET LAWS PASSED WITH LITTLE POWER

I n 2009, when I was just over two years into my political career, I launched a campaign for a private member's bill about the Holodomor, the Stalinist genocide of Ukrainians. Stalin had not only forcibly collectivized farms but stored enough grain to feed everyone then sold it for export. Millions of Ukrainians starved to death as a result. I credit one of our former Speakers, Dave Levac, with the idea for the first tri-party bill in Ontario, perhaps even in Canadian history. Dave was of Ukrainian heritage himself and was aware of the demand for action on this front. He was also cognizant of the fact that my riding included a large number of Ukrainians, as well as the biggest Ukrainian festival in Canada. For some time Ukrainians had been asking us both to act with a bill declaring that there had in fact been a genocide in Ukraine. Both Dave and I agreed. While he was still a Liberal Member, before he became Speaker, he suggested that we work together on a private member's bill.

Neither of us had success with the bill within our own parties. I needed Liberal support to get anything accomplished, and he didn't have enough clout to get his own leadership team's vetting. We managed to secure the support of Frank Klees, a Conservative, as well. Thus was tabled the first tri-party bill. It made great sense. Certainly, getting passage of a private member's bill that way would be easier we hoped. The idea of a tri-party bill was so new that no one in our respective parties said "No." We forged ahead. It had never been attempted before. The result was that it was one of the few that did become law that year.

Brilliant! Let's move on from here, I thought. I imagined all we could achieve if we used the same format. I followed up, as did others, and was part of several more bills to acknowledge various cultural and ethnic groups. For example, the Jewish Heritage Month Bill was put in place to celebrate the acheievement of Jews in Ontario despite often virulent anti-Semitism. A British Home Children's Bill was passed to recognize another victimized group, the British children sent to supposed safety away from Great Britain during the Second World War. Many were used as child labour. And there were still others. All were important, but pretty non-controversial. Then I started to wonder what might happen if I tried to get something controversial done using the same method.

Toby Dancer, who'd died while she was music director at Emmanuel Howard Park United Church, was the name I'd put on a bill adding "Gender Identity and Gender Expression" to the Ontario Human Rights Code as a protected entity. Many trans activists, including Susan Gapka, had been looking for an MPP willing to put forward a bill, and I was more than willing. I wanted to memorialize Toby and what better way than enshrining trans rights as human rights. We would be the first major juris-diction in North America to do so. It was time.

Toby's Law had been re-introduced time and again, after every election. The Government kept saying the same thing, "Trans rights are already cov-ered," even though the head of the Ontario Human Rights Commission, a Liberal, disagreed. Yet, the times had changed. Back in 1971, I'd been the only woman to sign the "We Demand" statement. By 2012, the list of actions called for in that statement were almost all won or partially won:

1. The removal of the nebulous term "gross indecency" and "indecent act" from the Criminal Code and their replacement by a specific list of offenses, and the equalization of penalties for all remaining homosexual and heterosexual acts; and defining "in private" in the Criminal Code to mean "a condition of privacy";

2. Removal of "gross indecency" and "buggery" as grounds for indictment as a "dangerous sexual offender" and for vagrancy;

3. A uniform age of consent for all female and male homosexual and heterosexual acts;

4. The Immigration Act to be amended so as to omit all references to homosexuals and "homosexualism";

5. The right of equal employment and promotion at all government levels for homosexuals;

6. The Divorce Act be amended so as to omit sodomy and homosexual acts as grounds for divorce; moreover, in divorce cases, homosexuality per se should not preclude child custody;

7. The right of homosexuals to serve in the armed forces, and therefore the removal of provisions for convicting service personnel of conduct/and or acts legal under the Criminal Code; further the rescinding of policy statements reflecting on the homosexual;

8. To know it is policy of the Royal Canadian Mounted Police to identify homosexuals within any area of government service and then question their sexuality and the sexuality of others; and if this is the policy, we demand its immediate cessation and destruction of records so obtained;

9. All legal rights for homosexuals which currently exist for heterosexuals; and

10. All public officials and law enforcement agents to employ the full force of their office to bring about changes in the negative and de facto expressions of discrimination and prejudice against homosexuals.

With Pierre Trudeau's famous statement that "The state has no place in the bedrooms of the nation," homosexuality had been decriminalized in 1969 federally, but that hadn't come close to ensuring equal rights for LGBTQ2S people. The "We Demand" statement outlined what would begin to accomplish equal rights. Trans, Two-Spirited, and queer people, however, were still omitted from our understanding. Nevertheless, what we'd asked for and seen as almost utopian at the time had been accomplished. We were still waiting on an official apology from the military when I tabled Toby's Law yet again (the military apology came later, in 2017), but we'd accomplished enormous change. It was time for trans rights.

Some four tablings later, having heard all the Government's excuses, I knew even they were beginning to cave. This time I tabled it as a tri-party bill with co-signatories: Yasir Naqvi, Liberal; and Christine Elliott, Conservative. The fifth time was the charm, and the tri-party format was the key. Those on the Government benches were afraid to see the NDP march with Toby's Law signs in the upcoming Pride Parade. They were finally sensitive around any perception of transphobia. Imagine that! We had come a long way.

Under huge pressure, the Government had just brought in a law necessitating the formation of Gay-Straight Alliances in schools just before we tabled Toby's Law; however, it was Peter Tabuns and I, along with a long list of queer organizations, who demanded these groups be called Gay-Straight Alliances and not hidden under a less upfront name. For the first time, the queer bashing and bullying that had always been present in our schools was being recognized as the deadly activity it was. LGBTQ2S kids were killing themselves. But prevailing attitudes were shifting. What had been seen as too revolutionary in the 1970s, even by queer revolutionaries, had become a possibility.

Toby's Law passed second reading in the same year, 2012, and I knew it would become law in time for Pride in June, a parade at which I was delighted to be named Grand Marshal. LGBTQ2S rights were making strides! The Government had already relisted sex reassignment surgeries in 2008, so that they could be covered by our Medicare system, another signal we were going to win. Again, our trans activists across the province were finally being taken seriously.

In the press Toby's Law, when it actually became law, was a tiny sidebar, though we were the only major jurisdiction in all of North America to have added trans rights to human rights. It should have been huge news. For the first time a trans person could legally resist being fired or evicted because they were trans.

Not being taken seriously is something women and trans folk understand. We were almost always sidebar issues. Domestic violence continues, however, and continues to rise. In 2019 almost four women in Canada were killed a day through domestic violence. In the queer community, sexism, racism, and transphobia are an issue. Gay men had become a stereotype as every girl's best friend in sitcoms and movies, but not so much lesbians. Straight male porn was where you'd find "lesbians." Bisexuals were invisible and trans roles, if they existed at all, were played by straight men. But who cared about the press? I was elated. Finally, Toby's memory was honoured and a human rights bill had become law.

The rights won by Toby's Law represented a major victory. The law impacted the way our entire province did business, everything from identity cards to prison practice. I don't believe for an instant that the Government realized the scope of that one change to the Human Rights Code. I'm glad they didn't look too closely. In the years since the bill was first tabled, it had moved from "fringe" and impossible to necessary. None of that just happened. All of it took concerted efforts of activists on the ground as well as political manoevering. The battle was won in increments.

Waving at the thousands at the Pride Parade that year perched on the back of a convertible, I ruminated that it had only taken me forty-one years of queer activism to get there. I didn't feel the slightest resentment. For most queer activists there is never an accolade and very often imprisonment or death. I was beyond lucky. Toby wasn't.

I held Toby in prayer that Pride year and wondered what she would have thought of it all. I wished she'd been there to witness third reading and then Royal Assent. A true introvert, Toby would have been profoundly embarrassed by the focus. Toby, who'd been so victimized. She was a victim of psychiatric, economic, and religious systems that were profoundly damaging. Toby had won that year and would never know it, but I like to think we'll meet again, and I can fill her in over some Cristal and laughs. Toby's actual ashes were always with me at the Legislature and are with me still. Passing that bill was way better than any memorial.

Since then some of her ashes have been strewn in Los Angeles at the House of Blues, at a drop-in for queer youth in Toronto called Toby's Place, and around various jazz and blues venues. Toby's stained-glass window is still at Roncesvalles United Church and trans folk still have their photo taken in front of it. A small commemorative plaque outlining Toby's Law is beside it. Very infrequently someone who knew her will call me, and even less frequently someone will ask for some of her ashes for remembrance. None of her family has ever inquired. We had become her family. Every trans person who exercises their trans rights in Ontario, and now in Canada, carries her legacy.

The $10 minimum wage campaign had shown me the importance of my new career, but with the passing of Toby's Law, I really finally understood what all the insanity had been for. I understood my calling. We could accomplish real change that affected real lives. In elected office you can gain rights for the marginalized and the vulnerable, even if you aren't part of the Government or even close. You just need to remember, as they say, "who brung ya"—you're there to serve your constituents. You have to be willing to work with your supposed enemies for the good of those who need action. Toby's Law might just save lives. It also proved the efficacy of the tri-party bill. If you could find just one member from each party to agree it was inestimably easier to get the bill to become law.

It will save lives. Adding trans rights—to be specific, "gender identity and gender expression"—to the Ontario Human Rights Code, gave trans folk the same human rights as everyone else in a jurisdiction of 13 million people. Governments across Canada and the US took note and more jurisdictions followed suit. Five years later, in 2017, the federal government followed and acted. The federal bill covered only federal employees who were trans but was an important symbol. Our bill had far more practical impact. It is little known, however, how much our law impacted housing, healthcare, and employment for all trans Ontarians. The change is still occurring. Toby, may you rest in power.

■

In the midst of working on Toby's Law and all the associated negotiations, I'd met with trans rights groups across the province, and another issue came to light: conversion therapy. TG Innerselves, in the Sudbury area, raised the issue with me in the course of our discussions. Conversion therapy is the practice of trying to turn queer kids straight. Most were aware of "pray the gay away" groups (predominantly Christian-Right) emanating from the U.S. The success these outfits claimed was all fabricated, including the conversions claimed by one of the largest organizations in the ex-gay movement, Exodus, whose president, Alan Chambers, finally admitted none of it had ever worked and apologized. Exodus had 400 chapters around the world before it closed.

I was naïve enough to believe conversion therapy wasn't widespread in our province. Yet, as we travelled around with the Committee on the Gay-Straight Alliances Bill, we heard testimony from a group of psychiatrists and others whose main practice was conversion therapy. They claimed success. It was truly terrifying. We were horrified that children were being subjected to that. Those particular psychiatrists were religiously based. Then, after meeting with TG Innerselves, I learned that the main intake centre for trans children and teens looking for support and perhaps surgery was also practicing a version of conversion therapy. One trans person who spoke at my press conference described her experience: a team of men in white coats had examined her when she was sixteen, and the head of the program accosted her with, "You're far too masculine looking to ever pass as a woman!" I guess the idea was to force trans children to run a psychological gauntlet before they were "allowed" to receive the medical assistance they needed.

Clearly there was a need to act legislatively. I immediately tabled a bill in 2015 to ban conversion therapy for youth and to delist it for adults under our Medicare program. No one should pretend it was efficacious or ethical. This wasn't trans-specific legislation, but they were the group still being routinely subjected to it in Ontario, and the practice was still widespread in faith communities. I knew I couldn't get all-party support for this bill, but the timing was right. Again, I tabled it just before Pride and immediately set to work lobbying Government members. The Liberals had a new leader, Kathleen Wynne, who is an out lesbian herself, and as a cabinet member she had helped when I needed it in the past. How would it look if the Liberal Government with the first lesbian Premier didn't act on this bill before Pride?

I had no idea how rapidly change could take place, and I thank many behind the scenes on the Government side with helping that process. For example, one Liberal, Emma Wakelin, who has since come out as trans, was working as a staffer back then. Primarily, though, I demonstrated there was political capital to be had if the Government acted, and a significant downside if they didn't. My own party's leadership wasn't happy about the number of bills I'd already passed, and they certainly didn't want to give me any more wins. Their justification was that the Government would allow only so many bills to pass from the opposition benches, and by pushing so many bills, I would steal someone else's success. After all, everyone had a bill they wanted to see made law. To me, however, this wasn't about political victory at all. The Government seemed more than ready to let the usual number of NDP bills pass as well as act on conversion therapy.

I recognized I wouldn't get the support I needed from my own team. It wasn't about me, though; I wasn't even going to run again. The facts were in: conversion therapy led to an increase in LGBTQ2S suicides. This bill was absolutely necessary to save children's lives. Political reality, however, meant playing sides against each other and getting the press involved again. I knew the House Leader, Yasir Naqvi, supported the bill, and I hoped the Premier was onside. They seemed to want this passed before Pride. I tried to make the case to my party that if the NDP didn't get behind the bill, we'd be mud when Pride season started. Bhutila was on maternity leave at the time, so Andrea Houston was my executive assistant. Andrea had been a columnist for *Xtra*, a queer weekly in the city. She knew the press and she wouldn't hold back. Still, the response I got from my leadership wasn't encouraging.

I remember a conversation with Yasir, who wondered, "Why isn't your own team supporting it?" I had no real answer. They did support it; they just didn't support me. I simply argued the merits of the bill and made it clear that if we acted, we'd be first in North America.

Still, I felt like I wasn't getting anywhere. I was caught once again between male leadership (two male House Leaders) who just wanted to arm wrestle. When the bill came up for second reading, there was no doubt it would pass, but something rather unusual occurred. The Premier, Kathleen Wynne, herself came to speak to the bill and vote for it. One of the Members, a 20-year veteran of the Leg, said it was the first time he'd ever witnessed a Premier showing up to support an opposition bill on a Thursday afternoon. The news spread rapidly. Our own leader, Andrea Horwath, then arrived as well to speak in favour of the Ban Conversion Therapy Bill. Fantastic! The Conservatives were a mixed bag, but the Liberal Government had a majority. We didn't need the Conservatives.

Near the end of each legislative year the House Leaders negotiate which bills will pass from Second Reading into law and which won't. I knew the process. I'd been the Whip once upon a time. I'd had too many wins, and my party didn't want to give me another one. That was our true hurdle in getting conversion therapy banned. This wasn't even a tri-party bill. Even those had fallen out of favour with all parties, who wanted wins with a partisan stamp. As stated, the Conservatives may not have signed on in any event. I had a fight on my hands. I recognized that the bill was in jeopardy if left to the men.

In the spirit of mutually assured destruction and after pleading with both sides on the issue, our only recourse was the press—again. Special thanks go to Andrea Houston, who lived through this frenzied time with me. We had limited days left before the House rose. An article appeared

in the *Toronto Star* describing the logjam and the fact that party bicker-
ing was holding up a bill that so obviously needed to pass. Say what you
will about tactics, but the end result was a ban on conversion therapy! Our
action even got a shout-out from then-President Obama, who cited it and
said that should be the case throughout the U.S.

In record time, a matter of weeks, the bill went to Committee after
working out the language with the Ministry of Health, and then into law.
The fastest win ever. I was a wreck by the end of it, but nothing I had ever
done in the Legislature was so worth the risk. If your team already sees you
as a potentially dangerous loose cannon, what real risk is there?

■

If there's one lesson here, it is that if you believe in what you're doing and
have a solid community base that backs you up, you can get an enormous
amount done. From this description of law-making, I hope it's clear that
politicians of all ideologies—even a member with no real power—can
make change happen. You might pay the price politically, but so what? The
reason you're elected in the first place is not your ability to "go along to get
along" with your own party. You are elected so that you can actually make
the world, or your little slice of it, a better place. Please remember that;
you'll regret it if you don't. Believe me, I've spoken to many ex-members
around the world, and the most common regret I hear is that they were too
much of a "team player" within their party and didn't get enough done for
their electorate.

■

When the Ban Conversion Therapy Bill became law, the institution that
had been responsible for practising a version of conversion therapy closed
that clinic and restructured almost immediately. The executive director
called me at home (how did she even have the number?) to let me know.
The doctor who'd been in charge of the clinic and others testified against
the bill at Committee, but by the Committee stage the battle is already
over. TG Innerselves came down to celebrate. The win was theirs.

As long as trans folk continue to live with almost 50 percent rates of
poverty and suicide attempts, there's more to be done. Now the real fight
has moved to education and enforcement of the rights won. Our children
are so vulnerable. That work is ongoing.

CHAPTER 19

SPEAKING OUT FOR PTSD AND FIRST RESPONDERS

Working across partisan borders worked with Liberals, but it also worked with Conservatives—surprising for a Socialist kid. Such was the case with my bill declaring post-traumatic stress disorder a workplace injury for first responders. Early on in my political career, PTSD came to my attention, embodied by a young queer woman, Shannon Bertrand, who'd been assaulted on the job as a paramedic. She'd been diagnosed with PTSD following the incident yet couldn't get compensation or even paid time off from work. Shannon had been asked to prove to the government bureaucracy that the PTSD came from her job.

When someone's career is lived out on the front line, a certain amount of stress comes with the territory and the old "suck it up" macho mentality was prevalent then—just power through it. The Canadian military had long ago understood that PTSD was as real an injury as any bodily wound and it compensated its personnel if that was the diagnosis, allowing them time to heal. First responders often had the same sorts of expectations placed upon them, sometimes even more intensely since there was no end to their "tours of duty." So PTSD should be seen as a workplace injury. No one should have to prove that—it's almost impossible to do so anyway. For first responders, multiple incidents are often involved and the traumatic effects are sometimes cumulative, arising long afterward.

The first iteration of the bill started with declaring PTSD as a workplace injury for all workers. But that wasn't going to get buy-in from the other parties—it was too broad. I approached the police and firefighters. It took many meetings, but the next bill specified first responders, including police, firefighters, and paramedics. Our files, meanwhile, swelled with cases of individuals who never got the help they needed and with many PTSD-related suicides. The unions immediately backed us, representing tens of thousands of members. The Government kept insisting that these workers were already covered by the Workplace Safety and Insurance Board, and refused to acknowledge the re-traumatizing experience it would be for someone forced to prove their mental injury to that Board was caused by their work. The precise source of PTSD was, in some cases, almost impossible to pinpoint.

One firefighter called our Queen's Park office saying he was going to kill himself. He'd been fighting with the Board for years and was unable to work. The irony of the call was that he insisted we not call 911. "I know those folks," he said. He didn't want to traumatize them by having them find his body. I explained to him that I must call, and ultimately that's what deterred him from taking his own life—that others would indeed find him. He didn't want his death to hurt someone else.

There was another irony, that this former drug-involved street kid was working for the cops who'd been her enemy. The reality was the police needed help, and no one was stepping up. I came to understand how impossible a job policing is. Since then I've been on record to defund the police and redirect money to community and social workers, who should be the ones to intervene in calls involving mental health and minor drug issues. In part, this is because of my work on the PTSD issue. I believe police are doing work that should never have fallen under their mandate. I also supported the Pride decision to remove uniformed police from the parade. Again, police management have to finally understand the way police have been used to terrorize street kids, Blacks, Indigenous People, and queers. The system we have fails everyone including those enforcing it.

I tabled and re-tabled the bill, working with colleagues from other parties, trying to get their support. Little by little, opinions were shifting. There is power in numbers, and having the support of all those unionized people made a huge difference. They represented voters and financial support. The bill was also clearly non-partisan. The Conservatives, who were always quick to defend police, were on our side from the beginning, giving it their public support. When the new Conservative leader, Patrick Brown, stepped into the House as leader, his very first question to the Government was "Why doesn't the Government make PTSD a workplace injury for first responders?" Even though he didn't acknowledge that it was my bill, his action helped the cause immensely.

My most ardent opponent in caucus, the same one who'd led the charge at that fateful caucus meeting where I was trashed for speaking out, called for applause for me for the bill. It was a darkly funny moment for me, but I took the support from whomever and wherever I could get it. I wasn't the only one in that room to see the irony.

Like most of my bills that became law, the PTSD bill finally went from being inconceivable to becoming a political necessity. A young police officer shot himself in a clear case of PTSD-induced suicide. The news put the Government on the spot. Not only did first responders demand action, but so did the public and the press. The Government rewrote the bill to include corrections officers and dispatchers, which we would have done anyway— remember, my first writing included all workers. That change allowed the Government to call it their own and, as would be expected the male cabinet member took the glory with a nod to me. No mind, PTSD was legislated a workplace injury, and we were again the first jurisdiction in North America of any size to make that change.

Most importantly, though it took multiple tablings, many years, and innumerable second reading debates, Shannon Bertrand, with tears in her eyes, was able to say she'd won! She had. Watching the press almost devour her asking for intimate details of her attack was unsettling, but even that she bore with the bravery that had brought her to my office in the first place. When the cabinet minister who had revised and tabled the final bill was given an award by an organization devoted to first responders with PTSD, Shannon and I were acknowledged as an afterthought. No real award for her. *This*, I thought, *is what it looks like for another sheroe, without whom nothing would have happened.* Humble Shannon never complained. This is what it takes to get help for those that need it most, but I was still saddened to not see her name engraved somewhere as the woman whose courage made it all possible.

■

I wasn't considered such a traitor in my own party after that victory, but I was always suspect. After all, it was staff and me in negotiations that made that policy happen. We got something done, again. By the end of my political career, in fact, I had passed more private member's bills than anyone in Ontario's history, and it's a long history including thousands of members. That realization made everything I'd been through worth it. Through smear campaigns, my party's shunning, the endless days, my own depression, and all the other crap, it was so worth it in moments like the PTSD victory. To witness Shannon knowing that all her suffering would finally be addressed. To know that the firefighter who called our office could finally get help. I was happy to work with Conservatives, a party I had nothing in common with ideologically, if that's what we could get done.

When tri-party bills were no longer allowed except under unusual circumstances, and the political atmosphere became even more about winning, the bloom had clearly fallen off elected office for me. The rationale was that every party wanted to have clear "wins." They didn't want to share those wins with anyone. In our party this happened a few years before I left politics in 2018. Rumour had it we weren't alone, and that management in the other parties felt the same way.

In a majority situation, how else but by negotiating with the Government could you get anything done? When opposition is just about making the Government look bad and yelling across the floor, the very real needs of those who elected us in the first place become secondary. In my experience, "winning or nothing" means nothing, not even winning. Our party's rank and file got that, but leadership seemed oblivious.

In the next federal election campaign in 2015, the federal NDP made exactly the same mistakes as the provincial party had. The party ran to the centre, speaking of balanced budgets, allowing the Liberals to seem more progressive. They got the same result that we had at the provincial level—they lost both the election and their credibility.

As right-wing populism grows into far-right fact-denial, the left also loses its ability to temper the damage if we can't find a way to speak across our political chasms. By all means, "Call the fuckers out!" as Kormos would have said, but it's just as important to keep talking to them. As it says in the Talmud, "To save one life is to save the entire world." It becomes necessary in every profession to remind ourselves that principles matter and, dare I say it, that we're called to "love our enemies." I felt so sorry for all my colleagues as I saw the realities of political life and public service wear away at the hopes that had brought them there in the first place. As I said before, no one should want a one-party state. Even in a dreamed-of socialist utopia, an opposition is needed. As the Soviet Union under Stalin proved with its totalitarian character, mass imprisonment, and murder, even in a system other than capitalism, you still need a real opposition. We become what we hate. Over and over, we do this in myriad ways both small and large.

Admittedly, it all becomes much easier if you're seen or are a little crazy and unpredictable. That way, wherever you find yourself, you can speak truth to power. As soon as you're terrified of anything—being fired, or losing your status, or even just being thought badly of—"they," whoever they are, own you. Bizarrely, political office is a rare post from which your boss can't fire you, and yet it's where people are most afraid of their bosses. No doubt, if you ask members who've been attacked by their own, they've found it devastating. But the job of the elected, whether within capitalism or socialism, is to do as much as possible for those who put their trust in you and to always work for the marginalized against the powerful. It may sound corny, yes, but your job is actually to work for the people.

First and foremost, that always means working to reform your own party. It is possible to do that. People have. The same member who led the attack in the infamous caucus meeting where I was denounced as a traitor later led the applause for my PTSD bill, and had said, "In union halls we battle like crazy, but when we walk out the door, we walk in solidarity no matter what the decision." I thought about what that kind of solidarity has wrought in history, with no whistleblower to curtail it, even in the union movement. That mindset has supported the fossil fuel industry and voted for everything from two-tier contracts, to misogyny, homophobia, and purges. Historically, that attitude has led to totalitarianism and to every kind of atrocity where solidarity among the few has destroyed the lives of the many. I applaud all the whistleblowers everywhere who say, "No, this isn't right," willing to point out that the emperor has no clothes. Many of them women. Many of them queer. Many of them thought of as crazy.

At the end we stand before the Divine, not before them. It is possible to resist.

CHAPTER 20
GIRLS AND WOMEN

While I was campaigning in all four elections, something became obvious to me. Young women seemed disconnected, uninterested in discussing issues or policies, whereas young men were engaged and eager. However, girls in the ten-to-thirteen age range in school were excited to see women like me running for office, and they wanted to talk. What happened to girls in their teenage years that silenced them?

The question is fairly easy to answer, really. If you walk into legislatures anywhere in North America, as girls do on field trips, you'll see portrait after portrait of men, but few women. If you watch the news, man after elected man speaks, but women not so much. Popular culture and media tell girls that their real job is to be beautiful, a desired object, and oh yes, they may have a career. If anything, the pressure on young women today is worse than what I experienced in the seventies during the second wave of feminism. Roles were clear then. Expectations for women were pretty low. We still heard that we ought to get married, have children, and be quiet. Now, girls are told they can and must do everything. They should get married and have children. But they should also look perfect and have professional careers, all in an unfair, racist, patriarchal world. Women are still paid much less than men. Women still inhabit the pink ghettos (beauty, childcare, secretarial work, etc.). Women are still not represented even remotely equally at boardroom tables or in governments. Girls aren't stupid. They see all this. They get the message about their futures, and for most the idea of going into politics doesn't even enter their minds. It goes without saying that it's far, far worse for non-white and trans women.

I knew I had a chance to help change that. *Let's introduce Girls Governments programs in our schools*, I thought. This was something I could do immediately, starting in my own riding. I wouldn't have to wait on any bill or law. We thought grade eight was the right time to start, before high school and hormones and ramped-up cultural pressure came more obviously into the picture. One of our public schools agreed, and once a month we held meetings with a group of girls selected by their principal. They learned some feminist political history, debated, chose a topic to focus on, and then constructed a campaign. We helped educate them about the levels of government, who was responsible for what, and tactics.

The carrot for the whole program was a behind-the-scenes trip for the girls to both our provincial and federal governments, highlighted by meetings with women in power who shared their stories. The entire thing was absolutely non-partisan. The girls had access to cabinet ministers, senators—people it was difficult even for Members to meet with. I was sure it would work because it was win-win both for the politicians (great public relations and photo opportunities) and for the girls themselves. Mutual benefit was essential to the program's success. The girls got to have a press conference as well, which was sometimes actually attended by the media, and occasionally they got write-ups in local to national press.

It would always culminate with all participating Members and girls posing with the Speaker on the Grand Staircase at Queen's Park. The girls even got to see inside the Speaker's apartment, which is in the same building as the Leg. Many Members have never been able to see inside that personal retreat!

Internships had happened before, but the goals of Girls Government were different. Interns often work for Members and there's no political payoff. There had to be something in it for both the girls and the politicians or it wouldn't grow beyond my office. Girls Government, on the other hand, was a bit of work for my staff and me, but it came with its own dividends. I knew other Members would love that too. The program began to spread across the province through other Members. For most, except perhaps the participants in Ottawa, the federal government visit was a huge deal for the girls. For Ottawa Members, the payoff was their trip to Toronto and Queen's Park.

Both male and female Members took up Girls Government at various times. All the political parties got involved. It was fun, and most importantly the girls seemed to love it. Over my years in the Legislature, all of the public schools in my riding were involved, some more than once, and almost always the girls said it was the best experience of their school year.

Equal Voice, our national organization that lobbies for just that—an equal voice for women in elected office—noticed and backed our program. The program was put in place across the province at various times and my hope was that Equal Voice would take it national. I still hope they will.

The public schools in my district ranged from upper-class enclaves in wealthy areas to schools filled with daughters of first-generation immigrants or refugees. Think of what it meant when they got to meet women who looked like them, who had the same background, and who were elected! I always encouraged the girls to ask any questions of the elected women they met. Nothing was off limits! One girl, the daughter of refugees, asked an elected Member, a young woman, how much she was paid. When the young woman Member told her that at that time, she was making $157,000 a year, plus perks, all the girls erupted with expressions of awe. "Whaaat?!" "No way!" That Member was a non-white woman in her early thirties, also the daughter of a refugee. The young girl who had initially inquired had never met anyone who looked like she did and made so much money. All of a sudden, what had previously seemed impossible to her now seemed possible.

If Members were out of town a great deal, their staff could easily run the in-school part of the program, and then the Member could welcome the students at Queen's Park and speak at the school. Members could easily change the format to suit their circumstances. It was all good, a win-win all around. Girls across the province chose topics ranging from the environmental to human rights to animal rights, and beyond. No matter the politics of the Member, the girls drew their own conclusions. The experience gave them tools. It provided introductions, too, for future summer jobs, internships, and even staff positions later on.

The problem with the more classic, civics class engagement at the college or high school level is that even if a Member visits the school, the kids never get to see where they work. In such settings, I have found that the boys tend to take up all the air at the microphone or in the classroom, and typically the girls feel silenced. Unfortunately, I've witnessed this phenomenon countless times and across class divides.

Girls Government rocks on to this day. Eventually, if it isn't pursued by others, it will not be because the girls don't love it but perhaps because the girls themselves put too much heat on their own representatives during question sessions. It might work a little too well. That's another advantage of the program!

■

While I had less success with another feminist initiative, it's still worth noting. I, along with a Muslim woman, Fizza Mir, and a Jewish woman, Francine Dick, wanted to take some sort of action on the issue of violence against women. Way before #MeToo, it was obvious that we were losing the war on violence against women. Domestic violence, in particular, needed more than a law-and-order response, which clearly wasn't working. As women of faith, we got that patriarchy, and its traditions in our own religions, was part of the cause. Not only were we engaged in rescuing the holiness in our scripture from those who would use it to hate, but we needed to do the same more specifically for women. We wanted to do something in our places of worship, too.

I'd met Francine through party circles. She had long been an activist on social justice issues. Fizza I'd met when, after 9/11, we had taken two actions at our church. The first was opening up the sanctuary all night so that people could come in and pray. Everyone then was terrified that this would be the beginning of World War III. All night people from near and far drifted in, lit candles, sat. Few anywhere were sleeping. The second action arose out of a concern for our Muslim neighbours. The local mosque was just blocks away. We invited all of Jami Mosque to worship with us that Sunday and to pray for peace.

That Sunday, an entire school bus of our Muslim community members arrived with their Imam. We had a moving multifaith service calling for peace, something that from that day on became an annual event at Emmanuel Howard Park United. It sparked evening meetings between the two faith groups as well, where we could learn about each other's faiths and ask questions. Fizza was a youth group leader at Jami Mosque at the time and she and I immediately recognized our common interest in justice.

My idea was to give the issue some political weight and launch the initiative from the Legislature with officials from our faiths present for the signing. We decided to call our fledgling organization Ruth's Daughters, after a piece of scripture we all shared. It comes from a story of a woman's love for another woman, in this case her mother-in-law, and their attempts to use the only tools available to them, their sexuality and their intelligence, to survive. There is no "God" foregrounded in the Book of Ruth. It is almost as if in telling the ancient tale, the author showed in the work the feminine face of the Divine under patriarchy. With all the men in their lives dead, the two women, Ruth and Naomi, had no hope for survival except begging and prostitution. They concocted a plan where together they would seduce a wealthy man, one who showed kindness, and because of him, survive.

It's a tricky piece of scripture because at its heart it's so awful. Only through a man could they live. Yet their loyalty and love for each other is also its pulse. Used in both straight and queer weddings, the lines, "Where you go, I will go; and where you stay, I will stay, your people will be my people and your God my God. Where you die will I die and there will I be buried, God do so to me and more if anything but death part you and me" (Ruth 1:16–17).

With Ruth's Daughters, no bill or motion was necessary. Instead, we used the weight of the Legislature to add importance to the launch of Ruth's Daughters as an organization with leaders of Muslim, Jewish, Buddhist, and Christian faiths in attendance and as co-signatories to our printed statement declaring that we were all against violence against women in any form. The idea from there was to start groups devoted to ending domestic violence in our places of worship and to get faith leaders to put their weight behind the initiative.

To prepare ourselves we invited women from a number of traditions to attend workshops on domestic violence at our local Victim Services branch. Mainly volunteers, they were the ones who accompanied police when a domestic disturbance call came in, going along to assist the victims (almost always women). Victim Services provided the training. We thought some of our women should at least get a taste of what that training looked like and an idea of how prevalent "domestics" were.

Our hope was that faith communities, or at least the women in them, would take up the cause and volunteer. Perhaps some might dedicate a service a year to the issue, or form ongoing support and activist groups. It seemed to begin well enough. I was attending a new church at the time. When clergy leave the church where they were in leadership, it's necessary to provide space for the new incumbent by attending elsewhere. But I had the backing of my new minister to try out a group, and we held a service to commemorate victims of abuse. Francine started a group at a Jewish community centre, and Fizza got together some women she knew who were active in mosques. Most inspiring, some Roman Catholic women started, and still hold, a mass on the issue.

That's when the depth of the problem became frighteningly apparent. Independent of religious backgrounds, all of our attempts to build something failed. Firstly, the leaders were only to happy to show up at Queen's Park and sign on, but few were committed to the followthrough. In fairness, some did try to initiate something, like the Roman Catholic women who started the mass. Most, however, did not. Secondly, Fizza, Francine, and I all had the same experience in trying to start our small groups. Women didn't come. I truly believed women cared, and I was baffled by the lack of response. One woman who came to a meeting spoke for many: "Our husbands think that in showing up I make it look as if I'm being abused and he's responsible." Independent of class standing, colour of skin, religious affiliation, or any other marker, women stayed away because of their husbands' concerns. They stayed away because of how it might look in their communities and/or because they saw it as someone else's problem. Women who were actually being abused were too terrified to come out. Naively we had believed the problem wasn't as pervasive as it actually was, but the issue ran deep. Dutifully we kept trying until it was obvious we'd failed. Or rather, I, as the originator of the project, had failed. I failed the most.

It was a lesson. The isolation and shame of abuse keeps women, all women, separated. I hadn't thought it through. Our churches, mosques, temples, and synagogues have services of remembrance and acknowledgement for a large variety of causes, mostly organized by women, but the issue of domestic violence is too close, too near, too real. Men, including those we love, are too close, too near, too real. It's too intimate. It's too uncomfortable. It's too dangerous. We can speak of it in the abstract or help our local women's shelter, but we just weren't ready to bring it home.

However, two wonderful programs were started, at least in part, because of the work we did. One, the Mass to commemorate women victims of violence, is done annually by our Roman Catholic Diocese. I still receive their mailings. The other, begun by Jewish Family Services, was to encourage synagogues to put notices in their women's washrooms with numbers to call for help. I saw one recently as I was visiting a Shul, and it was so moving. The women's washroom is a brilliant place to provide information, and the practice has now spread to bars, restaurants, and other places. Ruth's Daughters wasn't a total loss. Thinking back to my own rape experience, I think I understand.

I never had the courage to confront my rapist in person. For years I really thought, *what good would it do?* He was someone I cared for, family almost. When I finally did confront him, I did it by email. I didn't have the guts to do it in person. The sheer cruelty of his pretense about it was shattering. I think what is so difficult for women to understand is how someone who seems to love you, seems to care, actually, on some level, hates you. They see you as less than human, as a "thing." Rape seemed to me punishment for the crime I'd committed of simply being alive. After meeting up with the man again, I realized he wasn't a friend. In my pretending he was, I'd reinforced his own thinking that somehow I "deserved" the rape or that it wasn't rape at all. We never spoke again. After the last time I saw him, decades after the fact, I returned to my hotel and had two of the best martinis I've ever tasted. I was still shaking. All my bravado at the time it happened was just that. The experience was terrifying and it took me decades to recognize just how terrifying it was.

It also takes women to keep rape culture alive. I remember reporting a disturbing comment by a boyfriend to a woman I considered a good friend. Her response was, "Oh, he would never say something like that." Essentially she was accusing me of lying, indicating she would rather lose my friendship than see the man in anything but a positive light. Usually, that "nice" guy—that brother, husband, son, grandson, or friend—seems the last person who could ever be a rapist. We women defend them time and again, over and against our sisters. The great gift of this feminist wave of acknowledgement, exemplified by #MeToo, is that we are finally called to side with our sisters. We are called to take a woman's word over a man's, something we've been culturally conditioned never to do.

The other problem is with the justice system itself. A frontline rape crisis counsellor told me that she now advises women to not press charges. She said that, in her experience, the woman suffers, and the man usually goes free. How would it feel to see someone that we loved in some way in prison anyway? Of course, that's only if we could prove anything. Hopefully, we change the system, and there is much work to be done. Perhaps we can all start by acknowledging our own abuse and believing the victim.

Patriarchy still teaches women that if we are assaulted, it's our fault. We were too sexy, too defiant, too confident, too assertive, too something. On some level we still believe that's so. We, not our attackers, feel the shame. That is how we've been trained.

In the end this prevailing culture is why Ruth's Daughters failed. But then again, perhaps for me its success was on a personal level. I did send that email. It said simply, "You know you were the one that raped me. It was you." I pray most rape survivors get to say that, even if nothing else comes of it.

CHAPTER 21
ALL CREATURES GREAT AND SMALL

I t has been said that the real insight into the compassion of a society is how it treats its animals. Canaries tell us about coal mines. With breed-specific legislation, I saw how hysteria wins over science and can lead the political agenda. At one point everyone feared German Shepherds, then Dobermans, then Rottweilers, now pit bulls. As humans we've loved to fear sharks or spiders or wolves. All of this sensationalism masks the fact that we are, by far, the most dangerous animals. A few attacks by dogs, perhaps one or two, had led the news. If it bleeds, it leads. *Pit bull* even sounds scary. Reality demonstrates that any large dog or gangs of small dogs can maim or kill.

It's clear enough to anyone who thinks: owners should be responsible for their dogs' bad behaviour. Even the idiots involved in dogfight rings know this. So should we. In fact, those who breed dogs to fight simply move from breed to breed as fashions and laws change. The answer to dog attacks, from any breed, is twofold: education for the owners and for the rest of the public; and steep fines or criminal charges for those who use their dogs as weapons or don't comply. One by one, countries that had tried breed-specific bans (like Italy) discovered that the banned breed did less biting, but other dogs bit just as much. Of the 50 U.S. States, 21 have passed laws that in some way prohibit breed specific legislation.

Dogs and their owners organized around that unjust law and still do, but what about all the other animals? In particular, what about whales, dolphins, and seals performing in captivity, an issue brought to our attention in 2012. A wonderful trainer approached me because of the absolute cruelty he witnessed at a game park I still feel unsafe naming, for fear of being sued. In fact, we learned, and newspaper reports confirmed, that dozens of whales, over twenty dolphins and untold other animals had died at the park and were buried on the premises. The film *Blackfish* and stories emanating from some American sea parks also caught the attention of the media at the time. Every year when the park opens for the season, scores of demonstrators protest. I spoke at some of these demonstrations and held a fundraiser for the trainer to help with his legal costs. I heard one child say, "We're going home when the park closes. When do the animals go home?" The reality was that many of the animals went "home" into dank, dark cells. Profoundly social animals were left alone. We delivered tens of thousands of names on a petition to Queen's Park demanding action from the government. The *Toronto Star* ran a series of articles on the trainer and the situation.

One orca who had watched all her offspring die became the focus of a prolonged campaign. Zoocheck, the one real non-industry oversight organization, had said she was so far gone that there was really no compassionate way to save her. She was too old to be released into the wild and the best she or we could hope for was a transfer to a less cruel facility.

One would think any reasonable person, on learning these facts, would want to act. The problem was, of course, political. Local politicians often accepted donations from the park, and it offered employment in a region where jobs were scarce—even if the jobs weren't great and you'd be fired if you spoke up on behalf of the animals. The other overarching issue was that we had virtually no laws protecting these animals, and profoundly weak ones for other animals. As I dug deeper, I learned that while you need a licence for a dog or cat, there is no such condition for owning a whale or a tiger or a lion. Of course, authorities could get after you for other reasons if they wanted, but the reality is that they never did. When the OSPCA tried to charge the park with cruelty, they couldn't win because the laws were so inadequate.

The lack of action stemmed from an ethical problem in that animals, all animals, are seen as "property" and not as sentient beings. If they're property, then there's not much you can do to force the owner's hand in terms of care. Interestingly, a similar issue plagues environmentalists.

When Indigenous People or environmentalists work to protect the land against the large oil and gas conglomerates and others, their position is often based on the premise that whatever a piece of paper says about title, the land should not be desecrated. A few people should not decide on the health of something that gives life and is living. The same is true for animals. Neither flora nor fauna can speak for itself. Neither can vote.

In 2015 Quebec had managed to pass a law declaring animals as sentient beings, while still leaving all agricultural animals out. I knew the agricultural lobby fought and would fight against any law restricting their rights over the animals they owned. Omitting farm animals would be the only way to even begin a conversation about animal rights and protection, so no farm animals were covered by the law. Even though I asked for a bill identical to Quebec's with no farm animals covered, I could find no support for the concept, not even within my own caucus, never mind any of the other parties. The argument was that while farm animals weren't covered in the Quebec law, it was a slippery slope, and the farmers would fight it.

Times had changed at the Legislature and my early Wild West days of getting bills written, tabled, broadcast, and out to the floor without a fight were over. We, or at least I, could barely get bills okayed in theory. Political life would have been unworkable otherwise, but sadly the machinations effectively shut down initiatives that might only have been nixed by a few Members. In this instance, however, the process proved prescient. If I couldn't convince my party to support such a bill, I could be sure no one else would support it either. No one was willing to do much, or anything, for animals.

The Government "felt" the animals' pain, of course. That was just good public relations. Finally, after more than 100,000 signatures on petitions about the game park, the Government passed a law stopping them from importing any more whales. I was pleased with that, as were other activists, but it did nothing to help those already in captivity, nor did it diminish the ongoing abuse to other animals. My staff started calling me the "Critter Critic."

Animal activists across the province saw a sympathetic advocate and began letting me know of countless other campaigns. My social media feed filled up with horrendous pictures and stories of animal abuse, from farm animals to pets to zoo animals. Nothing had ever sickened me so much. It became a nightmare, and I had to ask them to stop because of the disgusting nature of the photographs. The gruesome images didn't help anyone's cause. Like violent pornography, the side effect of seeing such horrors can be that it inures people to the violence. Nonetheless, they were on the side of angels and right as to the extent of the horror. My reticence to know reeked of cowardice.

When you go up against the largest industries, you can expect little or no political support and little or no success. I'd experienced this phenomenon before but never to the extent that I felt it in trying, year after year, to draft something, anything, that I could get passed for animal rights. I would hear constantly how the agricultural lobby loved their animals more than anyone. If that were the case, then my simple question was, "Why wouldn't they welcome protections for their beloved animals?" The answer was always the same: it would be a "slippery slope" of regulation that would eventually put them all out of business. Funnily enough, I can think of lots of industries that should be more carefully regulated, whose lobbyists say exactly the same thing.

Politicians insisted they were looking out for their constituents, but animals are not constituents. It's a curse to know too much, as I discovered. In the process of simply trying to help a whistleblower, the trainer who tried to save an animal in his care, I came to know too much about not only our reliance on animals but also our abuse of and our complicity in that abuse of animals. It is virtually impossible to exist without using something, wearing something, or eating something that involves animal cruelty.

It's not unlike the oil and gas industry; you might try doing without your car, which is an essential in so many regions, but try doing without plastic. If governments don't act to stop abuse of animals and the environment with regulation from the top down, it will never happen. We're too enmeshed. The solution has to be a political response. The great lie, by contrast, is that by simply recycling, watching our own individual relationships to animal products, and making small changes, we can impact what goes on. Yes, we might make a dent, but those choices on their own will never solve the problem if governments don't act. I don't feel I was even hoping for much when trying to create a bill, just to replicate our next-door neighbour's legislation. But even that was too much. My inability to enact any legislative change in the area of animal rights remains the biggest regret of my political career.

Meanwhile I did try to change my own behaviour, eating way less meat, buying from ethical producers of cheese and eggs, and other local improvements. We've changed our habits at home markedly, but it feels like small stuff. I know it really doesn't amount to much. The lone orca still swims around in a pool, the equivalent of keeping a human in a bathtub until her wretched life ends. People still take their children to watch the cruelty, innocently maybe. Knowing what's behind the façade and being impotent to doing anything about it is difficult. To the animals suffering and the humans who care, I can only say, "Mea cupa, mea maxima culpa." My sin, my most grievous sin. I'm so sorry.

CHAPTER 22
POLITICAL CHAPLAINCY

Mondays, Tuesdays, Wednesdays, and occasional Thursdays, Ontario's provincial politicians huddle together over jumbo shrimp and copious amounts of booze. Lobby events were Members' dinners. Most barely know who's hosting and don't much care. These gatherings are a chance to eat, drink, and meet with colleagues from all parties, plus staff other than your own. One veteran Liberal Member referred to it, accurately enough, as "the trough." I found that often the best information, negotiation, and even affirmation came from the camaraderie of lobby nights. Almost everyone I knew in politics was either veering toward alcoholism or in recovery from alcoholism already. Lobby nights fed that too. We were all in need of what we clergy call "pastoral care," or care of any kind.

My own United Church was absent from the halls of the Legislature, any legislature, except maybe to make a visit every decade or so for some particular issue. In terms of care of the members themselves, most churches expect us to go to them, not the other way around. Considering most Members were not from Toronto, where Queen's Park is situated, there was little chance of that. But there was one lovely evangelical woman, another sheroe, who made it her mission to be present at House sittings. She contacted every Member with the simple offer to pray with and for them. Very few took her up on it, but I did. On all things theological, perhaps even on all things political, we probably disagreed. But these things didn't matter and never came up. Once a month we'd pray together.

Other denominations and faiths made their presences known from time to time too. Some had lobby days of their own. Others advocated politically, like the Anglican Archbishop Colin Johnson, who met with every caucus and asked how to get poverty on the agenda of the next election. I suggested all-party debates be held on the issue in Anglican churches. They actually did it. The result was profound and made a difference.

Those without a faith background really don't understand how powerful it is to have someone pray for you and to know that a community exists with only one purpose: to learn to love each other, including you. Those who do have a faith community and happen to be in elected office really miss that in the warring world of politics. It can be a very lonely existence. Other Members communicated their disappointment, and often depression, to me and to each other. It was an open secret.

My blood pressure had been inching up ever since I'd started political life. It's what killed my mother, affecting her kidneys and eventually her heart, and I took it seriously. I suspected that the core of the problem was spiritual. We'd all started out with such high ideals and hopes for reform. The longer we were there, the more we became used to the call of the party over principle or person. The longer we were there, the more the constant campaigning and stress over re-election got to us. It affected all of us engaged in public service. At my best, I felt phenomenal compassion for all of us in the Legislature. I still do. Feeling unable to tell the truth hurts your soul.

Then, as now, I was honoured to have so many search me out for what I came to call "confessions." I would never divulge confessions, except to say that most Members from all parties chafed under their own leadership, felt enormous amounts of stress at all times, and resigned themselves to settle for very little in the way of actual accomplishment. Many who'd been there a while wanted out but couldn't see how that was possible. It certainly wasn't easy. For most, returning to their previous profession would mean starting all over again, usually in middle age. One common dream was to work for a non-profit. One Member said they longed to "work for good instead of evil." There was a note of sarcasm, but a hint of truth as well. By the time I left, I was amazed at how many I heard express more or less the same sentiment. Every one of them would likely deny ever saying anything like that, of course. Again, when you're unable to tell the truth, it eats at your soul.

It seemed to me we all, from all parties, had an ethical call: if you don't like it, change it. I'd been very critical of our federal leadership's campaign in 2017 the one that mirrored our provincial move to the centre. I was one of the first to say I thought the federal leader Tom Mulcair, should resign. Remember, I knew I couldn't be fired. When he was more or less voted out and did resign, I felt it was incumbent upon me to step up. When I announced that I would run for federal leader, I had no expectation of winning, but I truly wanted to make some political arguments. I wanted to speak for the many in our rank and file who longed for someone to say the word *socialist* and fight for the party's socialist values. Many in our ranks wanted our party, which seemed to have drifted so far from its roots, to reclaim its early ideals. We needed to demand free tuition, free child-care, Pharmacare, increased taxes on the wealthy and on corporations, and even—gasp—worker control of key industries. That's what socialism means. Why wait for someone else to say it?

Everyone thought I was crazy. Hey, that technique had proven effective so far. As ever, I didn't care about winning. I very much hoped that someone else would take up the banner and free me to return to church work. I actually spoke to Avi Lewis in the hopes that he would consider it. Sadly, he declined. After the last crushing federal defeat, I and many in the party felt it was important for someone to state the obvious.

That Pride, I marched with the banners about all the LGBTQ2S bills I'd managed to get made into laws—more than any other politician in Canadian history, as we found out later. Pride, as usual, was hours late and the day was brutally hot. As we came to the end of the route many, many hours of standing and waving and walking, later, I felt faint. That was unusual. I'd been hydrating all day.

The only other time in my life I'd fainted was when I was very pregnant with my son. At that time, I was standing on the bus with five-year-old Francesca, and Don was at work. I knew I was going to pass out, so I quickly found a kind-looking woman and asked her to look after my daughter. Then I collapsed. I came to in an ambulance later with Francesca and Don staring at me with terrified expressions.

At the end of the Pride Parade route, I sat down on the curb to try to get my bearings, but the sensation didn't pass for many minutes. Looking back now, I'm not sure if I lost consciousness or not. After a little while, I felt stronger and was able to drive home.

More disconcerting was later, when I had the same experience at home, doing nothing more strenuous than watching television. I felt not only numb but, worse still, in trying to call out for help, I also couldn't get my mouth or voice to work. My speech sounded garbled. That terrified me. I suspected a stroke, and I was right. I drove myself directly to the hospital. Insane, yes very, even though I live close to one. Many tests and appointments later, it was determined that I'd had one or more TIAs, transient ischemic attacks, or mini-strokes, but luckily no brain or motor damage. The solution was an adjustment to blood pressure medications and baby aspirin, and, needless to say, medical advice to lessen all stress. It was time to quit the race.

Luckily, I knew another woman I thought might run, Niki Ashton, who shared my socialist aspirations and felt the same way about politics and our party as I did. She had placed third in the last leadership race. This time I threw my support behind her, and I believe in her still. I lived in hope. I live in hope. As Marx said, the alternatives are "socialism or barbarism," and it seemed to me that barbarism was winning. As long as that is true no one with a conscience can sit at home and not act. For me, though, for the good of my health, it was time to take a step back. I'd already made it clear to my staff right after the last election that I wouldn't run again.

Like so many who have walked this path and been honoured to serve, I began to look forward to a life post-politics. I was one of the lucky ones. I knew where I wanted to be, and I had a reasonable expectation that I could find a "calling." I'd done some work for a Washington-based diplomatic service that certainly paid better than the church, but it wasn't where I was meant to go. It took almost twelve years at Queen's Park before I knew for sure, that what I really wanted was "the best job in the world": Ministry. I longed to return to church. I missed the human environment—not utopian, but human. I wanted, finally, to go home.

CHAPTER 23
THE RADICAL REVEREND

efore I was first elected I appeared on CIUT 89.5FM, now the only non-profit community radio station left in Toronto. I started my own show on the same station around 1998. My offering was called *The Radical Reverend Show*. I really wanted something on the air waves that focused on the left hand of faith, progressive religion, and leftist politics speaking of faith. I knew such a reality existed, yet the airwaves and television were dominated by the Christian Right. I loved the radio format. It was possible to highlight those who were rarely heard, queer Muslims like El-Farouk Khaki, but also those who were heard but then not well known, like anarchist David Barsamian, the host of *Alternative Radio* out of Boulder, Colorado. I produced and hosted and really only relied on the station for technical support (even there, my son, Damien, teched for me for years). I found the voices not heard on mainstream media interesting to speak to and about.

After taking some time off to settle into political life, I restarted the program as *Three Women*. It was more political and represented women with a range of opinions, political, and other. Organizations that couldn't find a woman to represent them on the air were out of luck. I'd started at CIUT as a part of a feminist collective, and I was delighted to keep feminism on the air. We had callers and emailers, and while on the campaign

trail I'd hear from dedicated fans who'd listened to the show for years—
always a pleasant surprise at the door.

The radio show was also helpful in pushing forward progressive
bills for the queer community and others, too. Any of my bills, like the
Ban Conversion Therapy bill, or Cy and Ruby's Act for Parent Equality,
had activists on my show speaking about the bill's importance and why
it should pass. With the PTSD bill, I highlighted paramedics and other
frontline workers. Our animal rights activists from belugas to pit bulls
had their turns, all on *Three Women*. Every woman I've highlighted in this
book has appeared on either *Three Women* or *The Radical Reverend Show*
at least once. I had to keep it non-partisan but it definitely veered left. After
all, we were an "alternative" radio station.

At various times, my guests have included numerous MPPs; the
Premier, Kathleen Wynne; the now-Deputy Leader of the Conservatives,
Christine Elliott; the NDP Leader, Andrea Horwath; countless MPs,
including Chrystia Freeland, now Deputy Prime Minister of Canada,
Niki Ashton, and others; and Toronto City Councillors and lots of activists. CIUT has a large broadcast range, and our program goes out to half
the province of Ontario and some of the northern US states. We're also
available online and now on podcast. During my time in politics, just
when I'd think no one was listening, I'd knock on a door and come across
someone who said they listened all the time. I'd always respond with, "Oh,
so you're the one!" No matter what our audience numbers were, lots were
actually tuned in and contributing.

I've been on air now for more than twenty years, and I must say, the
politics and challenges of community radio itself have been fun. We've
had two station managers accused of significant theft, a number of political coups for various reasons, numerous run-ins with authorities over
everything from swearing on air to the political views expressed. We even
hosted Canada's largest radio station, the CBC, when they were locked out
on strike. Money, or rather the lack of it, is always a concern, but astoundingly we keep hanging on, supported by listeners and students. During
the turbulent times, two dedicated individuals proved to be the backbone
that kept the radio broadcasting: Ken Stowar, who became station manager; and Sam Petite, who, with soldering gun and duct tape, kept the
machinery going.

As producer and host of my own show, I've had some hiccups too. Once, when my guest was a no-show, I ended up interviewing myself. The joys of live radio! That was fun and is still remembered. I've hosted every kind of guest imaginable, from a "Rapture Specialist" to a stoned-out kid who was convinced they'd met God. All were fun but the most meaningful to me are always our activists.

After leaving politics I reverted to *The Radical Reverend*, which now podcasts, too. As far as I know, no other show highlights the left, progressive religious perspective for all faiths. We give space only to those who are LGBTQ2S-positive. And as I repeat often, "The Christian Right is neither." Regressive religion is a major source of evil in our world. Even if I'm not in party politics anymore, I will always be political.

These days, we're in a groove where we have a political panel called "Left, Lefter, Leftist" with a Marxist, Alex Grant; a Left-Liberal, Emma Wakelin; and me, of course. Once a month we have a queer show, featuring the likes of Susan Gapka, Andrea Houston, and many others. There's also a "Law and Disorder" panel, where we discuss defunding the police and the Black Lives Matter uprising, and where guests have included Black advocates and authors Andray Domise, Joshua Michael Sealy-Harrington, and Sandy Hudson, and a faith panel with, among others, Rabbi Aviva Goldberg, Annie Matan, and Fizza Mir. My new producer, Jake, another angelic person sent when I needed one, makes it all sound seamless.

One of the groups to appear on my show frequently has been Students for a Free Tibet. My riding was home to one of the largest Tibetan communities in the world outside of Nepal, and they fit in well with our theme. They also taught me much about non-violent resistance. Tibetans are a population mainly in diaspora after the occupation of Tibet by China in the 1950s, that are up against the largest and arguably most powerful nation in the world. The few against the many. Or, at least the government of the many. Toronto has a population of about five thousand Tibetans, yet if the issue of Tibetan autonomy comes up, we can count on hundreds of Tibetans to congregate on the front lawn of Queen's Park with 24 hours' notice. At their community centre, which was built by the donations of a mainly refugee population, a thousand or more will gather for significant celebrations. They also support a camp for young Tibetans and others to train participants in the art of pacifist resistance.

The Tibetans I worked with, groups like "Students for a Free Tibet," were also savvy politicians. Hollywood had taken up the cause, with the likes of Richard Gere and the Beastie Boys backing "Freedom for Tibet." The Tibetan struggle for freedom was part faith and part politics and a perfect cause for this Radical Reverend. Our own government at Queen's Park was pretty pro-Chinese at that time, but our local Tibetans were realistic. They had never demanded no trade with China. However, they did demand that those who traded with China press the case for human rights for both Tibetans and Chinese, and for Tibetan autonomy. Tibetans were experiencing a kind of cultural genocide in Tibet, with language rights erased, mass arrests, and the rule by Han Chinese. To say nothing of the branding of their spiritual leader, the Dalai Lama, as a "terrorist." None of this, sadly, has changed for decades.

When it came to our attention that the then-Premier Dalton McGuinty, was going to be meeting with a high-ranking Chinese government official visiting Toronto, it was time to take action. I read a statement in the House demanding that our Premier ask about the lack of human rights for Tibet and the Chinese people. We in the NDP, asked that our government issue a statement. Predictably, they refused.

On the day the Chinese official arrived for the meeting, hundreds of Tibetans had gathered on the front lawn at Queen's Park. Many women had shaved their heads as a sign of despair over the meeting. Most upsetting for the Government was the presence of international, not just Canadian, press on the front steps of the Legislature, there to cover it all. Later that day in the House, understanding that the Tibetan protesters and the press were not going to leave until they did, the Deputy Premier showed me a statement upholding the human rights of all Tibetans that was immediately, unanimously adopted by the House. Now that's what activism can do!

Great thanks are owed to my executive assistant, Bhutila Karpoche, a Tibetan. With her leadership, she and I started the Ontario Parliamentary Friends of Tibet and an annual lobby day with information on the occupation along with music and terrific Tibetan food. OPFT is a sister group to the Federal Parliamentary Friends of Tibet. All parties come to the lobby day and also attend various celebrations at the Tibetan Cultural Centre. What the Tibetans understood was that non-partisanship was essential to their success in the Legislature. I have had the great delight of meeting His Holiness the Dalai Lama on numerous occasions and having a private audience with him on at least one, during which we mostly laughed and chatted about how strange the political process was. At one point he stated that he might very well be the last of the Dalai Lamas, or that perhaps a woman might be the next one. Certainly the combination of his leadership and the Tibetan people's focus on liberation through non-violent action has been profound. I still find Tibetans to be the best current example of faith and political activism combined with intelligence and compassion.

■

As I planned my political retirement, I was surprised and delighted when Bhutila announced that she would run in my place. She won handily in an election that saw the party sweep Toronto, after the Liberal collapse. The Ontario NDP ran on an entirely different campaign that election, a better one, and with an entirely different set of circumstances, the crashing of the Liberal Party in Ontario. Bhutila's victory was the first political win for a Tibetan anywhere in North America. It was history making. We were all thrilled. After eight years working with me, she entered the political arena with eyes wide open as to what she was undertaking. I had been such a novice by comparison. It felt like a wonderful transition. Not only was the district in good hands, and not only would my staff keep their jobs, but most importantly, in Bhutila the party had someone new who would continue to challenge the status quo. All very good indeed.

Both my radio experience and my exposure to the very real and substantial policy of non-violent resistance was a good training ground for how to work across difference toward a desired goal. The radio taught me that if you don't hear what you need to from mainstream media, you can always be your own media. And from the Tibetans I learned that non-partisan lobbying, a singular focus, and a commitment to non-violence can bring a cause affecting a relatively few people to the forefront of the world's attention. The fact that both exposures ran concurrently with my elected life at the Legislature influenced how I tried to circumvent partisan hostility, or "the war" if you will. Nothing new in this, of course, but I needed help. It reinforced my Christianity, the idea that you should "love your enemies." Even if, in political life, it's sometimes difficult to tell enemies from friends.

CHAPTER 24
QUEER CRITIC

Parent equality was something I thought we had for same-sex parents, but there was a significant loophole. Two very able initiators and allies, Jennifer Mathers McHenry and Kirsti Mathers McHenry, brought the issue to my attention in 2015. At that time, before I tabled "Cy and Ruby's Law" (named after Jennifer and Kirsti's two children), a sperm donor had more rights in our province than one of the children's very real mothers or trans parents.

When Jennifer was delivering her baby, she went into maternal distress. It was serious. As Kirsti told it, she was afraid Jennifer would die. That's when it became clear to Kirsti that she, even while legally married to Jennifer, had no legal rights to their newborn. Though same-sex marriage had been legal for years, no one had ever worked out what that would mean for parents. The horror of possibly losing your wife and then having a sperm donor, potentially uninvolved, able to assert rights to your child was incomprehensible—and should be. Both Jennifer and Kirsti were lawyers, and they understood the legal aspects of the solution. Yes, Kirsti could legally adopt her own children, but what kind of equality was that? Why should lesbian or trans parents have to jump through those costly and bureaucratic hoops? Heterosexual parents had no such challenges. That wasn't equal rights.

They were right, and it was an obvious bill for me. I'd been named the NDP's LGBTQ Critic, the first ever LGBTQ Critic in the Legislature. I knew we could solve this, and I drafted the bill. The problem wasn't with the ideas in the bill, but rather, as always, it was political. Neither my party nor the government at the time wanted to give me another win. I'd managed to pass the Ban Conversion Therapy bill by playing every card I had, including calling in the press. I couldn't replicate that. Not only that, but our bill opened up a number of statutes and laws that would also need amending. It was a legal can of worms.

My first stop was again the Government House Leader, Yasir Naqvi, a lawyer himself who had assisted me on banning conversion therapy. He suggested that we get lawyers from the Attorney General's office together with Jennifer and Kirsti. He also made it clear that unless my party fought for it, the Liberals would bring it in as a Government bill. It would become his bill. So be it. I didn't care who wanted the credit, as long as we got this legislation passed. The Government was feeling the Pride pressure, and as always the flurry of activity culminating in a new Law for same-sex couple rights happened just before Pride.

Outside the Legislature, Kirsti and Jennifer were actively promoting the bill as well. Other lawyers, other parents, folk in the community, all knew about the issue. We wore buttons. We held a protest. We circulated a petition. I made it clear that I didn't care whether the bill was passed as a Government bill as long as it became law. My party, and all parties, wanted partisan wins, but they didn't seem to get that who initiates a bill is a matter of historical record. Voters can be made aware of the facts. They can be informed about who started the challenge and why it was necessary—government inaction. Not to mention, there was no support from within my own party. For me again, that is, not for the bill. Without Government support, the bill and the change represented, would have died.

Of all the bills I ever tabled, Cy and Ruby's Law had the most lawyers involved. Many lawyers, both government and non-government, hashed out the details over so many hours. My role was to make sure they kept on meeting, kept on working to get it done. We had a deadline. It was just before the summer recess and the session was coming to an end. My aim was very simple: lesbian and trans parents shouldn't have to adopt their own children for the protection of their rights to be made legal. As you can imagine, issues of surrogacy, donorship, and gender all played a part in the final product. In the end, the lawyers came up with wording that we thought satisfied and covered everyone. (Years later, a male couple explained to me some small detail we had overlooked that had made it more difficult in their personal case.) Parent equality was at least as messy a sausage-making process as any law, perhaps messier. As usual, we had to settle for the most good for the most people. Yasir Naqvi tabled the bill, and we all celebrated when it became law, even if it had a straight man's name on it. I was just pleased that someone facilitated getting it done. We weren't the first province to gain full equality, but it was an important law I'm proud to have fought for.

■

By comparison, my Trans Day of Remembrance Bill was a breeze. It was the last bill I tabled before leaving the Legislature, and to this day no other large jurisdiction has such a law. It demands that all members in the House observe a moment of silence each November 20, the Trans Day of Remembrance, before Question Period commences. We chose Question Period because it is the time in the Legislative schedule when the greatest number of Members are in the House. The Trans Day of Remembrance was also the final tri-party bill I passed, and clearly the impetus was mine. It was a powerful reminder to everyone that among minorities, trans people are most at risk and have an unacceptable rate of suicide and murder. For years we had observed the day with a flag raising on the grounds, something we in my office had initiated. The bill added weight to the day.

In a way, I took it as a farewell gift from all the Members in the House. By then I had made it public that I was retiring from politics. I wanted to make sure that the day was honoured after I was gone. Who knew what the next government would look like? In a sense, the benefit of the tri-party process was that down the road, no matter who held a majority, their party name was on that Law, making it immensely more difficult to undo.

After I left, the next government to form was a Conservative majority, and with a profoundly Conservative leader, Doug Ford, who took office on June 29, 2018. Yet when I returned to the House for the Day on November 20, the Members still rose to observe the moment of silence—because it was the law and because their parties had signed on. The new government was in the process of dismantling much of our progressive work in the province, but my LGBTQ bills, all of them, held. In November 2019, the

Conservative Government even hosted a lunch in their caucus room for all the trans allies and activists that showed up. Imagine that!

■

Tri-party bills are so important in that they bind all parties in a government to the law, if passed. They also allow third parties, or even individuals, to influence law-making without much, if any, political power. These bills give activists without money and lobbying status, some say. Democracy, such as it is, becomes more democratic, not less. Certainly we proved out of my office that even bills still as globally controversial as trans rights can be made law using the tri-party bill format. Another example of this—and also of how important issues can be fought, won, and then undermined— was "inclusionary zoning." Inclusionary zoning is the measure some jurisdictions use to get affordable housing built without spending tax dollars. The Government simply enacts legislation forcing developers who build on a certain scale to set aside a portion of their units or houses that are required to be affordable, either gearing rent to income or forgoing down payments, or anything that brings that unit into the affordable category.

Though the practice was never popular with developers, I argued that as long as the playing field was even and the law also covered their competitors, it wouldn't be unfair. Developers had made a fortune in our province and in the City of Toronto over the decades. Inclusionary zoning, I argued, could even help them in a down market because at least they would get something for unsold units. If inclusionary zoning were in place, say 10 percent of any new builds over 50 units, 10,000 affordable housing units would be added in a year in Ontario. Those numbers would make a significant dent in our waitlist of close to 200,000 families, some of them waiting for decades for an affordable place to live. Successive governments had ignored the crisis, and as a result, homelessness, which was but a small problem when I was born, had mushroomed into a national disaster with thousands sleeping rough, some of them dying on our streets. Meanwhile, the option of a home, so readily available to my parents' generation, was out of reach for most. Even if municipal governments tried to make developers include cheaper units, with the way the laws were set up, the developers could appeal to a provincial body under the planning act and win. My bill would change the planning act so that municipalities could do the right thing. Many cities, which were paying for homelessness, wanted to act but couldn't.

If passed, the legislation was enabling, not prescriptive. The backlash to it showed the neo-liberal lie for what it was. Not providing housing was never about the money; it was about appeasing wealthy developer donors or not allowing one's opponents to benefit in any way. When the government said "saving tax dollars," what they really meant was saving tax dollars *for the wealthy*, not for the middle or working class, who were shouldering an increasing amount of the tax burden. Certainly it did not, in any way, assist the marginalized, the unhoused. Inclusionary zoning legislation with teeth would provide housing without tax dollars being spent at all! There was, and never was, an excuse to not act on it. Soon only the wealthy would be able to buy homes large enough to raise families.

As with the parent equality bill, the trans rights bill, and others, I knew who would listen on the Government side. I knew they were fighting about the housing issue even within their own cabinet. My strategy was to push from the outside, ask questions, and get press and public momentum so that if a cabinet member were to take up the fight, they would have external support if nothing else. Often a minister would approach me requesting I ask them a question on an issue I was pushing so that they could get more truck in their next cabinet meeting. I was only too happy to oblige if it meant getting one of our bills moved forward.

I made it a habit to give ministers the questions at the start of Question Period. It was an approach I copied from John Tory, now Mayor of Toronto but then Conservative Party Leader. By providing the question a little in advance, you could be assured of a more coherent answer. The question still had clout, but a little notice stopped the "gotcha" aspect of Question Period. Humiliating ministers didn't help anyone. Watching someone fumble through their notes didn't lead to positive change; it just satisfied partisan ego. On the other hand, getting the best answer a minister could provide showed us their arsenal and led to better strategies for moving issues forward. Again, what is the purpose of political office? Is it to get something accomplished for the constituents or is it just to humiliate those in power? To what end? So that you maybe, might, someday, win? Trust me, your adversary will always return the humiliation favour if you do manage to win.

I am a socialist, and I have lots of problems with the way parliaments and republics are structured, but that's what we have now. If we're privileged enough to find ourselves elected to one, it's incumbent upon us to do whatever we can to ease the burden of the thousands we were called to assist. I don't believe there's an either/or to politics. It's not either revolution or incrementalism. You work for both. What progress we've made has been while fighting for both. And we have made progress. Ask any woman, queer, or racialized minority.

So, with inclusionary zoning, eventually the Government had to bow to pressure. After all, they weren't going to spend any real money on housing, and this would be one of the only ways to provide any. I was there for the announcement and received the obligatory compliment from the Housing Minister Ted McMeekin (again, a man), for my years of tabling and re-tabling the bill. Nothing against Ted, one of the nicer cabinet ministers and a United Church Minister, but when someone asks me about patriarchy and politics, I think of all the times that a bill, originally mine, passed with a man's name on it. It felt to me like the inscriptions in all those male-authored books, "None of this would have been possible without the support, work, editing, room and board and sexual largesse, etc., of my [insert *wife, secretary, lover*]." Joking, perhaps.

Sadly, a Member's unwillingness to share what little glory there is often results in poorer legislation. In the case of inclusionary zoning, the law we ended up with had the kind of problems developers could still happily work around. Inclusionary zoning is still not in practice in Ontario. My conclusion is that no one really wants to provide housing. If they say they do, as Sir Walter Raleigh said, *then give them the lie*. I recall again my interaction with the other Housing Minister, John Gerretson, when I pointed out it would cost less to put homeless folk in hotels than in shelters, and that actual new builds would ultimately save actual dollars. His answer was "Yes, it's true," followed without pause by "Next question?"

He knew. We knew. I want to believe he would have loved to put billions into building housing, but would never ever get the green light from his leadership ("the Premier and a couple of twenty-three-year-olds") or the developers who contributed hugely to his party. In politics, money talks—and very loudly.

CHAPTER 25
IN RECOVERY

Leaving politics is like getting clean from methadrine—and I can compare. Politics is a series of exhilarating highs and depressing lows. It's a rollercoaster in a world of constant surprises and brush fires. Everything seems more important than perhaps it is. As with methadrine, berserk becomes your normal. The life is all-consuming. When you're going full speed on speed, anything else doesn't feel quite like living. And there's a comedown.

Finally, after twelve years of elected office, four challenging election campaigns, an incredible degree of success with issues I cared about, the desire for action rather than conflict, winning rather than negotiating, the rightward drift of the political conversation, and, finally, two mini-strokes, I was ready to change course. My first love had always been Church and I longed to return to a community where you didn't necessarily have to like everyone but you did need to love them.

I watched a few Members retire, whether they lost their seat or simply got out, and it often wasn't pretty. The death rate was high. Even if someone is a small fish in a smaller pond, fading into relative obscurity still felt, for many, like being forgotten completely. Those who transferred into another field and kept active fared best. I was lucky, some would even say blessed.

I knew what I wanted to do. I wanted to go home to the best job in the world. Church called. I met with the United Church personnel coordinator and asked what vacancies were coming up. He gave me the list and asked me to rank them. There was no question which church I wanted. It was the church known as the pre-eminent social justice pulpit in Toronto.

There were bigger churches with vacancies, but none with the reputation of being a centre of activism that Trinity-St. Paul's United Church and Centre for Faith, Justice and the Arts has. Years back they'd made a wise decision to convert their sanctuary into one of the city's top music venues, and they had become home to the internationally renowned Baroque music group Tafelmusik, as well as a number of other groups and artists. Their building, rather than being the drain on resources that most faith communities struggle with, made them income. This financial security freed them up for activism.

Trinity-St. Paul's had also been queer inclusive long before the United Church began to ordain openly queer clergy in 1988. One couple in our congregation, two men, celebrated their 62nd anniversary together the year I joined them. They also had an amazing music program and choir, led by a terrific director, Brad Ratzlaff. Over a dozen staff on the building side were overseen by another wonderful manager, Kendra Fry. They kept the physical plant humming along and our tenants happy. What Trinity-St. Paul's needed was stability in Ministry leadership. For one reason or another, they'd had eight clergy in ten years.

The Church describes the hiring of clergy as a "call" process. This one truly was. That the opening even existed when I was ready to take it seemed meant to be. The congregation and I were on the same page. And as it turned out, my first choice matched their first choice, me. Usually the process takes a while, but I received the call from them astoundingly quickly.

I'd told my staff at the last "victory" party, when the party had all but two seats in the entire City of Toronto, that this would be my last term in office. When it comes to political fortunes, no one ever knows what to expect, and I wanted to give them a heads-up so they could all plan their lives. I also didn't want to force the party or anyone into a by-election situation. I made my decision to join Trinity-St Paul's about eight months out from the next general election and timed the announcement so that everyone could relax until the general election (as relaxed as the pre-election period ever is). Bhutila, as I've said, was acclaimed as the NDP candidate in our riding, and for me it was the first time in eleven years I wouldn't have to campaign. Glory be!

My next order of business was to plan my covenanting service at Trinity-St. Paul's. The covenanting service is a time when both congregation and clergy make promises to each other for the length of their relationship. It's a marriage of sorts, and certainly a celebration. Kathleen Wynne, the first lesbian Premier, would preach at my service. I'd asked and I was delighted when she'd accepted. I suppose it was predictable, but some saw Kathleen's participation as a "fuck you" to them (as one Member so eloquently put it). What they failed to note was that I was entering a post-partisan world. They also missed that having the Premier of any political background preaching at a covenanting service was unprecedented. It was an honour for me to have her there. Everyone was invited, and scripture was read by members of my party as well, so all were represented. What they would really never understand is that I no longer had to "hate" my political enemies, whether Liberal or Conservative. For the first time in over a decade, it was expected that I would serve everyone and love everyone even if, as I said frequently, I didn't have to like everyone. The church was full, the service attended by press, politicians, family, and friends, representing ideologies of all varieties. It was a joyous occasion.

What follows is a sermon I preached a short time after beginning at Trinity-St.Paul's. It is emblematic of many. I called it "Not Your Bible— *Our* Bible," and it's based on the Beautitudes, with a goal of making them clearer to those mired in the "hate your enemies" world. There were many who found my move back to the Church incomprehensible when I could have run and won again in politics. I include it here in its entirety because I hope it explains the shift to those people, and to those who find church itself incomprehensible.

"Blessed are you who are hungry now, for you will be filled."

These and the rest of the Beautitudes are some of the most beautiful lines in all of scripture. Beautitudes after the Latin for blessings. They're also the most unsettling if we actually listen to them. Particularly the Lucan version with its "Woes" section. But then again, it depends on who you are. It depends on whose Bible this is, who this book belongs to.

I remember in politics, very much like advertising, the audience of key messages is very specific, often given a name, a gender, detail. This person is based on polling results as your party's typical voter. Ours was a woman, middle-class, college-educated, with 2.2 children. I always wondered about the .2 child? Question is, who did Jesus have in mind when he was preaching that day? Who was his target audience?

"Blessed are you who weep now for you will laugh. Blessed are you when people hate you, when they exclude you, defame you, on account of the Son of Man."

So, I can imagine if political parties or ad firms had a meeting about this target audience, our consumer of Jesus's message is hungry, crying, hated, excluded and defamed. Wow! What would the product be for such an individual? Fast food, an anti-depressant, a dating site, and perhaps a good lawyer?

But the crowd that huddled around this itinerant Palestinian Jewish rabbi was in need of something none of the above would help. Not just in the year AD that there were no anti-depressants, fast food, or dating sites. Lawyers, yes, the world's second-oldest profession. Even lawyers, though, wouldn't have helped them really. After all, they didn't help their rabbi, did they.

The target listener was alone in a crowd, suffering, marginalized. I like to picture the queer kid, the person from another tribe, those with disabilities, the women. I also thought of the crowd much, much later that must have heard these words coming out of the mouths of their owners, slaves. I thought of our own Indigenous and how they must have heard these words come out of the mouths of their colonizers.

Certainly, they weren't the words of the slaves or Indigenous. Slaves arrived on North American shores, with a variety of spiritualities. Indigenous had their own faith when colonizers and missionaries arrived. What did they hear from this strange book telling of a Middle Eastern reality so different from their own experience, and for that matter, so different from their oppressors? No doubt Christianity was forced upon them, yet there was something in these words both groups made their own. Something they heard preached, even out of the mouths of their murderers, that spoke to them even though the language itself was transmitted at the point of a gun.

Slaves passed along the words as they worked, sang them, shared them. According to scholars in African American studies, the Beatitudes were among their favourites. I think when you hear them it's obvious why that is. The words are seditious. They call to resistance and revolution. Even today, 80 percent of African Americans claim Christianity as their faith. In Canada, 49 percent of our Indigenous population claim Roman Catholicism, and 25 percent are Anglicans, despite the horrors of residential schools and genocide. In fact, today, both groups are far more Christian than their oppressors are. Maybe there was something in this strange book that spoke to them, something their enemies never meant for them to hear?

Dietrich Bonhoeffer, visiting the U.S. in the 1930s, when it was a profoundly racist and segregated country, said that Black churches were the most Christian in their worship, of all the churches he attended. They, I'm sure, were about as different as possible from the Lutheran Church he was used to in Germany. He witnessed a very different Church. So, it is with Indigenous, First Nations; their Churches are very different. Their Jesus looks very different. But they all listen to these same words.

"Woe to you who are rich, woe to you who are full now, woe to you who are laughing now. Woe to you when all speak well of you."

Truly these words are a condemnation of power. You would have to be comatose to not hear the Book speaking against the reader, as the master and the colonizer spoke these indictments against themselves. What they, the slaves, the Indigenous, must have heard—was hope. They were not alone. Wherever those strange words came from, whoever first said them understood what it was to be enslaved. Someone understood their own lives.

I remember in the midst of a brutal by-election campaign when I dropped into the evening service and dinner at my old church, a man I knew wrestled with crack addiction asked me how the campaign was going. I told the truth. I said, "It's awful. The smear campaign against me is hurting those I care for most. They're using my past drug involvement against me. I wish I'd never run in the first place." He responded with, "Blessed are you when people hate you, when they exclude you."

I know an angel when I meet one. Those words I heard that day from his mouth were written for me in that moment, for that time. Those words were written for anyone who feels oppressed, abused, marginalized, anyone who suffers, hungers, who is so alone. They speak of a justice not of this world but of the world of Christ, that world made real just in the hearing of them. Even vastly privileged me, in comparison to many, I understood that when I was most at risk, the Bible was my book.

The "woes" as well must have been heard by anyone with ears. How can you read the Bible any other way? All the texts of terror, of slavery, of misogyny, of homophobia, show themselves as very human and historical aberrations in contrast to the great sweeping epic of the liberation of slaves in the Torah and in the life and words of Christ. Those who are oppressed hear the liberation, the love, the promise. This is their book. It was written for us when we need it most. Those who have it all don't need the Bible. Those who lack, who have been humbled, see it as food, as community, as possible joy. Through every attempt to harness it to the will of empire, to the aims of the master or the colonialist, we can still hear the words of Christ come through.

There will always, of course, be those too who attempt to keep the good news to themselves. But it doesn't work that way. Loving one's enemies doesn't work when we do that. In the only truly effective resistance, non-violent resistance—the only course that doesn't turn victims into victimizers—there is no less understanding, no less desire to overcome cruelty. Working with Tibetans taught me that, even if we didn't already have the very Christian example of Rev. Dr. Martin Luther King. Tibetans, as the joke goes, are the baby seals of international diplomacy. Under the tutelage of His Holiness the Dalai Lama, they hold fast to non-violence against the largest nation on earth. They have always maintained they have nothing against the Chinese, not even their leaders, only their policies.

I've never met such a unified, galvanized people and there are so few of them in diaspora. I used to say at rallies, there was no question they would win their homeland back. The only question was *when*. I believed that because they have managed to win the support of those on the left and right of politics. News doesn't cover the fact that over 160 Tibetans have self-immolated. I remember the self-immolation of the Vietnamese monks and how that helped end the Vietnam War. To choose that, rather than killing someone else, changes those who witness it.

Early Christians, too, listening to Jesus that day, were tortured, imprisoned, crucified, while preaching non-violence and love. It changed their enemies too. Their enemies learned what love in action looked like. Love overcame death. Love for one's enemies is the kind of revolution that wins over armies and adversaries because you can't help but be changed when you witness it. Love of one's enemies prevents the endless cycle of violence the world witnesses. We are, all of us, witnesses as Christians to how that works. It's called Easter.

"But I say to you that listen. Love your enemies, do good to those who hate you, bless those who curse you. Pray for those who abuse you."

This is the farthest call, by the way, from masochistically abiding the hate. It is every bit as radical as the preferential option for the poor in the blessings. Who can accomplish this? Who can go on organizing, praying, rejoicing, growing, while acting in such an unnatural way? The simple answer is those who are assured they cannot lose. They are assured they will triumph. Not in some distant utopian future, but immediately, now. Those who experience blessedness in the vilest of circumstances and resist because of it.

Jean Genet, a queer French novelist and playwright, spent most of his life in prison and often had to write his novels and plays on toilet paper. Genet made of his prison, of those condemned to death, a work of art. His fantasies of the condemned covered in flowers, his ability to turn abject squalor into not just survival, but beauty, inspired none other than Jean-Paul Sartre to call him "Saint Genet." Which, in many ways, Genet was. In loving those who hurt him, in transforming the hell in which he found himself, he overcame shame, the flipside of pride, and won his power back. His work won compassion back for all those imprisoned. Both pride and shame are isolating and defeating. The profoundly ugly system that had taken his freedom could not force him to become ugly too. He willed to be beautiful. That is victory. Not then, but victory now.

This section of Luke asks us to do the impossible. It asks us, in the power of Christ, to be Christ-like. We undoubtedly will fail, but what a set of aims! Fail at them over and over. Fail bigger. Fail better. Just as we failed at the Ten Commandments, this gives us even loftier goals. Fail at these too, says Jesus, but try. Try.

Imagine again the target audience listening to the rabbi. The advice must have seemed incomprehensible. It still does. Who says those things? What manner of human says those things? Where do those words come from? It is as if we can feel something breaking open inside our souls as we hear them. Some barriers giving away. Some interior enemies surrendering.

"If anyone strikes you on the cheek, offer the other also, and from anyone who takes away your coat do not withhold even your shirt. Give to everyone who begs from you, and if anyone takes away your goods, do not ask for them again."

Sheer madness. I can imagine Jesus's audience holding their coats and what little money they may have just a little tighter. "Oh no you don't," they were thinking. Yet like a viral social media post today, they couldn't unsee the speaker nor unhear what was said. Truly earth-changing in its implications. Yet written for them, who in the final analysis had the least to lose. This would have meant the purest form of communism to be sure. This was the radicality of heaven.

These were their words, and this was their Bible. It didn't belong to the Romans nor to the priests or pundits. When Jesus lived those words in the flesh and died tortured, and so very young, it is no wonder that they and the disciples sold Him out and scattered. They should have known that was what would happen if you lived out those words. That's where those words lead one, isn't it?

But wait, here we are two thousand years later, and we're still listening to them. There are so many other activities we could have engaged in this morning rather than listening here to these words. But we are here. We're here still listening to the words of the itinerant Palestinian Jewish rabbi. If you look around, you won't see any Roman centurions. That whole empire is dust. There are still pundits and priests to be sure, those who would dismiss these words, or belittle them, or simply ignore them. But no mind. You and I are here listening to the Great Commandment: "Do unto others what you would have them do to you."

We, who have our moments when we feel so alone. We who hunger. We who question the world as it is. We who doubt. We who fear. We who lose hope. We who go into the streets resisting. We're still here. The rabbi is still preaching to us.

Still, two thousand years later, it's still our Bible after all.

CHAPTER 26
FOREVER THE YOUNG RADICAL

When I first walked into Richmond Hill United Church so long ago, the minister who greeted me, Rev. Ken Gallinger, said, "When I was in my twenties and first went to seminary and newly ordained, I was considered the 'young radical,' and now that I'm in my sixties and about to retire, I'm still the young radical." I say "Amen to that!" I might add that, when I walked into the Young Socialists' Friday Night Forum wearing a sheer sequined jumpsuit and six-inch heels, I was truly a queer socialist, and I'm still a queer socialist.

My story, in part, is a story of discovering an ancient faith to be inclusive of me, in fact, life-giving for me, just as I am. I always was and came to learn what I could be: I was called to be a queer woman minister. The socialist me discovered in the Bible, a book of revolution, liberation and empowerment, gifted to us by our ancestors. It is an open text inviting interpretation, theory, mysticism, and action. It terrifies and it awes. I love it. There is nothing more thrilling than to read a passage I thought I understood and find something completely new in it. The Bible is a communal work, written by many and meant to be interpreted in community. The community of faith attempting to live out its radical and different way to live, is still at odds with the world as it ever was. It's ultimately the community of faith that changed my life. This is the story of how that happened, with sex, drugs, trauma, and joy thrown into the mix. Most of all, joy.

Faithful queers and queer faith are my family. Politics and social justice, activism, was and is simply another ministry, another calling. Nothing is surprising to me when I look back upon this astounding journey. At my queerest I'm a person of faith. At my most faithful I'm most queer. There's no separation. Never was.

■

The story of Jesus's life seemed personal to me. Jesus was a queer, misfit rebel. Christianity fit me, not because of church but in spite of what I knew of as church. I knew Christ while high, during sex, on the streets of the city, in queer community, even while being raped. The music that spoke to me of Christ wasn't church music. It was the Stones, Dylan, funk, blues. I hadn't even been to church. Church was irrelevant until much, much later.

Much later I discovered that Jesus said in Matthew 19:12, some two thousand years before Lady Gaga, that some are born that way. Jesus was speaking about eunuchs, commonly believed by commentators to be those men forcibly castrated so as to be safe slaves around the patriarch's women. Essentially, Jesus was saying some men from birth had no desire to have sex with a woman. Queer talk. There was so much more that confirmed my early faith, but it took some discovery.

John, for example, was the disciple that Jesus loved. John was often portrayed as feminine, as in Leonardo da Vinci's well-known *The Last Supper*. Numerous historians like Sarah McNamer and James Hall have catalogued this. McNamer, in particular, describes the desire in the middle ages to portray John as an androgyne. Interesting. Reading scripture through queer eyes revealed some wonderful "perversions," rebellions that allowed me to take it seriously.

Interesting, too, that the first convert in Acts is a eunuch and Black. Philip is reluctant to baptize him because eunuchs were seen as sexually unclean by religious Jews. The eunuch persists, however, and history is made. (Among other writings on the subject, see F.P. Retief, "Eunuchs in the Bible," *Acta Theologica Supplement* 7, 2005)

In *Paul on Homosexuality* (Tubu Publishing, 2011), Michael Wood does an extensive exegesis on Paul's supposedly anti-queer admonition in Romans 1:18–20, debunking the assertion Paul was anti-homosexual. Wood is far from alone in reclaiming Paul. After all, in Galatians 3:28, Paul seems to question all binaries with "In Christ there is no male and female." Whatever you might think, Paul's writings, like the rest of scripture, have to be read in context. Paul does, after all, advise slaves to stay slaves in the Epistle to Philemon. So, should Christians support slavery? Certainly, at one time the Philemon text was used in exactly that way.

Social Gospel theologians like Ben Smilie and Liberation Theologians like Gustavo Gutierrez have shown people can and should read scripture as the story of the oppressed from the point of view of the oppressed. I argue, in *Qu(e)erying Evangelism* (2005), that we can and should read scripture through the eyes of the queer.

Genesis 1:27 says God created humans, male and female, in God's image. Could that imply a queerness at the heart of divinity? The story of Sodom (from which we derive the word *sodomite*) and Gomorrah, I discovered, cannot be read as a treatise against homosexuality. It deserves some exegesis. Let me use it as an example of how what is actually written changes what we think we know about what is written.

Genesis 19 starts with two angels entering the town of Sodom to test the town's faithfulness. Lot immediately recognizes them as both strange and different, if not angelic, and treats them appropriately as custom (and God) dictates, with hospitality. Before the angels can rest, a gang of men surround the house demanding the strangers be released so they can "know" them—or rather, gang rape them. Clearly, we should already see this is not about sexual desire. This is about assault. It is rape. The attack is based on the fact that the angels present as strange and different. Were they effeminate? What made the "appropriate" vigilante punishment rape, and not death or banishment? Suffice to say, there was something about these angels that the men thought rendered them less than equals.

Lot then says, "I beg you my brothers, do not act so wickedly. Look, I have two daughters who have not known a man; let me bring them out to you and do with them as you please; only do nothing to these men for they have come under the shelter of my roof." (NRSV, Genesis 8) If this passage were about sexual morality, since Lot is the ersatz hero, it would seem to say that when it comes to gang rape it's all right to offer up your daughters but not strangers. If we are to take anything at all from this story, let's hope it's not sexual ethics! Genesis 19 doesn't get any better as we read on.

In Genesis 30, after God had destroyed both Sodom and Gomorrah for their sin of not welcoming the stranger, Lot, having escaped, finds himself living in a cave with his two daughters who "know" him and produce offspring with him. If this is a sexual morality tale, we are to infer that incest is fine, and gang rape of females is fine; only a gang rape of a stranger, a man, is not.

The trick here is that the passage is rarely presented in its entirety. It has been, and continues to be, used as a "text of terror" against queers. Using a queer reading, this story carries, in fact, the opposite message. It's a pro-queer tale about how we should treat those different from us, particularly those we perceive as different sexually. We should treat those who are not gender normative as if they were angels.

The misuse of the story of Sodom and Gomorrah is a case of what theologians call *proof-texting*, or the propensity to take a few lines out of context. It's also indicative of what all theologians do, prioritizing those passages that they believe are central to the great thematic movement of the entire corpus of the Bible. In short, depending on who you are, what you represent, you pick and choose what is less important (as contrasted with more important) biblically. Those who see queerness as sinful read Genesis 19 one way. Queer theologians read it differently. Prove your case.

The book of Leviticus is often referred to by those who believe there's something un-biblical about queerness. Leviticus also has a rule against eating shellfish (9:10), but we don't often see demonstrations outside seafood restaurants. Even its admonition against men who lie with men (Leviticus 20:13) specifically calls for those men to be put to death. Thankfully, these days it's rare to hear even the most homophobic preacher calling for the death penalty for queerness. Also taboo are tattoos, mixed fabrics, animals of different varieties grazing together, planting different seeds together, and on for 859 verses, few of which are followed or even known. Why should one adhere to one of these and not the others?

Two other compelling examples, abortion and marriage, illustrate why knowing something about what the Bible actually says is important. Overwhelmingly the fight for access to abortion has been seen as a secular versus Christian issue, yet scripture contains not one word about abortion. Not one. The sacred union between one man and one woman has often been cited as Biblical. George Hayward Joyce in *Christian Marriage: and Historical and Doctrinal Study* (read Books, 2007) is one of many historians and scholars who have written on this topic. To condense much biblical scholarship, never mind simply reading scripture, monogamy is not the preferred form. Although not mentioned in the New Testament, polygamy was still practised by Jews during that time, in stark contrast to Roman law forbidding polygamy. Josephus, historian of the era, speaks of it as does Justin Martyr. They confirm that the normative practice was polygamy, not monogamy. It wasn't until the second or third century that Tertullian began to insist on the Roman Law demanding monogamy. Certainly, Jews of Jesus's era did not believe their law forbade it—quite the contrary. To them, scripture condoned polygamy; simply read the Hebrew Scriptures. Again, knowing this text helps dismantle some of the arguments against equal marriage promoted by those who see only one form of marriage acceptable.

This is how the discipline of theology has proceeded. Martin Luther, the great reformer, called the Epistle of James an epistle of straw. "My reasons are as follows. First: flatly against St. Paul and all the rest of scripture it ascribes righteousness to work..." ("Word and Sacrament," *Luther's Works*, vol.35, Fortress, 1960). Luther, famous for opposing the ability to work yourself into divine favour through good deeds or buying indulgences, wanted to make the point that the great theme of scripture was "salvation through grace alone." Only through Jesus's self-giving love, as evidenced by His crucifixion, was sin eradicated. Grace is given, not earned. If earned, Jesus's sacrifice was meaningless. Luther rejected James's Epistle because it didn't fit in with what Luther saw as the great overarching theme of the New Testament.

We and all preachers, readers, theologians look through our own lens. In reading scripture, a book written by hundreds of humans over thousands of years, we pick and choose. What is a faithful retelling of divine grace? What fits with the grand narrative? Queers can and should read the Bible as queer-positive. I would argue that the grand narrative for Christians centres on that singular moment where divine and human meet in the persona of a first-century Palestinian Jew who brought a message of profound forgiveness and grace. Someone who spoke truth to power and died because of it. Life wins over death. Love meant even loving one's enemies. Everyone is included in divine love, even you and even me.

Whether we like it or not, atheist or not, scripture has had and will continue to have a profound influence over our lives. It also carries extensive socio-political significance. Scripture will be used by those seeking or resisting power. The hot button issues separating left from right, like equal marriage, abortion, pacifism, are inevitably argued on a biblical basis by someone. We all need some education in what is written in the Bible and what it might actually mean. The Bible can still kill or save, and it does.

I learned over my life that someone could actually be queer and Christian. Since 1988, when I walked into the United Church for the first time (when their General Council dropped the prohibition against non-celibate gays and lesbians), I kept reading. I had always felt Christian but not religious. After 1988, I knew I could be both.

I also learned women clergy were possible. In Romans 16:1–2, Paul writes, "I commend to you our sister Phoebe, a deacon of the Church at Cenchrae, so that you may welcome her in the Lord as is fitting for the saints, and help her in whatever she may require of you...." Phoebe is a leader of her Church. In Romans 16, Paul speaks of Prisca or Priscilla, as she is known in Acts. In Acts 18:26, we hear, "He began to speak boldly in the Synagogue but when Priscilla and Aquila heard him, they took him aside and explained the Way of God to him." In Romans 17:7, Paul writes, "Greet Andronicus and Junia, my kinsmen and my fellow prisoners. They are prominent among the apostles and were in Christ before I was." Junia is another woman and apostle. In Matthew 28:8–10, Jesus appears after the resurrection to women first and gives them the task of proclaiming the resurrection and communicating this with instructions to the disciples. Women were, and always have been, evangelists.

■

You can take the kid out of the streets, but you can't take the street out of the kid. I'm still a survivor, and there's nothing laudable about simply surviving. I've been profoundly lucky, others not so much. Other women not so much. Other queer women not so much. Other trans women not so much. Other racialized women not so much. Almost all we women have achieved together has been paid for at a pretty steep price. Now I watch a whole new generation, those like Bhutila Karpoche and others, throw their bodies and souls into the fray, and I marvel. I always hope they'll suffer less, win more, change the world. I know, however, with the wisdom of hindsight, they'll probably suffer the same, win some, but still—I hope— change the world too. Together we've changed the world. We should rejoice in that. Boys often get the credit. Got it. We women are still willing to do the work, and nothing will stop us, nothing will slow us down one little bit.

We rejoice in our boys, too. That's also part of it. I think of Tommy Douglas, who brought Medicare to Canada. He made the world of politics work for the people who elected him. Of course, we thank the amazing sons, brothers, fathers, uncles, and grandfathers who have changed the world and been feminists too. Lots of books have been written by them and about them. But I hope that in these pages I've held up the other reality, a woman's side, as it were. I'm one example of a story that's repeated around the world, every day. When women tell our stories, we're often accused of speaking too loudly, saying too much, tooting our own horns, but here's the thing—someone has to! Someone has to say the emperor isn't as well-dressed as he thinks he is. We know. We make the clothes.

As I finish writing this book, in June 2020, the world is gripped in the COVID-19 pandemic. We're all under house arrest. This pandemic shows, as did the plagues of early scripture, just how governments and politicians and the corporations they serve have failed. One scripture of this season is John 20:19–31, where Thomas—erroneously translated as "doubting"; no, just *considering*—touches the wounds of the risen Christ. He then acclaims the words of the faithful always. "You are alive."

The touching of the wounds is very sensual, very personal, very real. We can imagine the blood still drying, Thomas's fingers recoiling at the pain the wounds represent. We can picture them both. This terrifying but also moving moment of great love. Our world's wounds are now apparent to anyone who sees. No more questioning allowed. Sir Walter Raleigh's "lie" will surely be invoked if anyone tries to deny it, either church or state. We have teetered, and will continue to teeter, on the edge of calamity, whether it's this pandemic or the climate crisis, racism, or the endless cycle of wars and occupations. This was so in Jesus's day. It is so now.

What wounds there are. Wounds of greed over compassion, underfunding healthcare, privatizing long-term care, refusing to build housing, allowing banks to gouge and profiteer in times of crisis. Wounds of believing ourselves to be in any real way separate from "them," the Chinese, the Africans, anyone, anywhere. COVID-19 has ripped back the curtain so that we can't pretend anymore. What happens to my sister happens to me. My sister lives everywhere and is everyone. She is of every religion, every skin colour, every class, every nationality. Unless she is healthy, we will all become sick. This is a soul sickness, every bit as damaging as a sickness of the body.

Thomas carries with him through the centuries the message that unless you see the wounds clearly, unless you face the blood and the sepsis and the stench of death, you'll never get to witness the Risen One. The Divine speaks to us through woundedness, too.

This will pass for now, but more plagues await us unless we release those who are captive. Those who are homeless, hungry, sick, abused. The ones I preached about that Jesus addresses in the Beautitudes. The ones the Bible exists for. Our enemies aren't humans, of course; they're far more pernicious and long-lived than mere mortals. Our enemies are ignorance and fear and the ideologies of money and greed. For people of faith who read their holy texts, none of this is new in any way. Neither is the answer to fear and ignorance. To conquer these devils, we have to keep educating, reaching across chasms of difference, loving those we see as enemies. We must always resist. We must always speak truth to power so that power gives way to people.

I happily took up my role at Trinity-St. Paul's Centre for Faith, Justice and the Arts. As the political world around us becomes more polarized and frightening, it seems to me the shift toward communities of support becomes more and more important. As we face crises, faith grows more necessary. There really are no atheists in the trenches. Everyone needs sanctuary even if it's virtual. We need prayer, even if it's online. That's the powerful, beautiful role of inclusive faith communities. I start every Sunday service off with the same words:

> Whatever you believe, whatever you don't believe. Whatever you've done, whatever you've left undone. Whoever you are and whoever you love, you are welcome here. Because this is not only the domain of the United Church nor is it only the domain of Trinity-St. Paul's, this is the Church of Christ and in Christ's Church, everyone is welcome.

Everyone means everyone. After all I was welcomed just as I was and am. Evangelism isn't about converting people. My intent isn't to convert anyone. Fuck it. Only the Divine can do that.

Just as the early community never expected a Messiah in the form of a Palestinian Rabbi, neither should we expect the next messenger to necessarily be Christian. People sit in our pews with a range of opinions and beliefs. Ironically, those differences make us profoundly Christian. Differences about Jesus, God, what is meant in scripture: it's all clear in the history of Christianity. Theorist Slavoj Žižek speaks of being an "Atheist Christian," also possible. Of course, I'm still a socialist, no contradiction with my Christianity at all. We include our share of supporters of capitalism too. There's always hope. Both politics and faith taught me it is essential to speak across the chasm of difference. We need constant reminding that no one should want a one-party state. I fail predictably often at that and at loving my enemies, as do we all. It's a journey, not a destination. Once, after we had a guest preacher who was pretty clearly a leftie, one congregant suggested I should include in my opening, "No matter who you vote for..." Too true.

My job as a minister, as I've often said, is the best job in the world. I'm honoured to be with people in the worst times, like pandemics, to the best times, like weddings. From devastation to joy. My week sees me wrestling with scripture and then speaking words I either hate or love, but words that have shaped our reality. I still get to be a social justice activist and don't hedge my comments, not that I ever did much. I don't miss political office. Truly, though, I have nothing but respect and compassion for those who dedicate their lives to trying to make a difference despite everything. I admire the change makers and support those individuals that stand on principle. They do exist and I thank God for them all. The "Radical Reverend" continues to be radical, if sometimes irreverent, both on radio and off.

I wear a collar whenever I'm on the job and that's a lot of the time, and in a lot of different settings. When I was first ordained, I wore a collar and a lovely old man greeted me with, "Good afternoon, Father." So gender-bending! The collar also manages to make both left and right uneasy, theologically speaking. I like that. The right wing thinks only a man should wear one. The left wing thinks no one should wear it. For hundreds of years, women wanted to wear one and weren't allowed to. I wear it for them, too. No matter which way you look at it, wearing the collar still retains shock value.

I return to Queen's Park now and sometimes get evicted over egregious acts of the new Government. (I have always been friends with the first woman Sergeant-at-Arms, who ushers me out.) It's important to be a presence, like a ghost, at a lobby day, or even to host a press conference. One press conference took place to ask the United Church of Canada and the provincial government for an apology for threatening my licence over the first legalized same-sex marriage and for the Church not having defended me and my congregation. Amazingly, speaking up got action! In one of the Liberal Government's last acts, they officially apologized. I've included their statement in the appendix (see page 211). The United Church of Canada, to this day, remains silent on the subject.

■

It seems fitting to end this segment of the journey by revisiting the stories of some of the women who, whether they know it or not, profoundly changed my life. For example, what ever happened to Paula and Blanca? Those two remarkable women, in the most natural act in the world—falling in love with each other—helped change the reality across North America. For years we three rented a convertible for Dyke Day and Pride and waved to the thousands who lined the streets, me walking while they rode on the back like two homecoming queens. Looking beautiful, as always, they basked in deserved attention and love. At one point, Paula was even asked to co-host a Latin talk show. They were media darlings—everyone's darlings, as they should have been.

After many years we lost touch with each other until I ran into Blanca in a local park. Over time and under untold strain, Blanca and Paula's marriage dissolved, and they are no longer together. It's understandable, really. They drifted apart. The homophobic expectation is that unless same-sex marriage lasts forever, it shouldn't happen at all. In fact, what happens to almost 50 percent of straight couples happened to them too. What is amazing is that same-sex marriages last as long as they do in light of such prejudice and hatred! When I followed up with Paula, she sent a short message. It was one of sadness as one would expect: "Painful..." she described it. As I write these words, I pray for them.

As for Toby, her ashes now sit in my office at Trinity-St. Paul's. I still think of her often and am so glad that her name is immortalized both in the stained-glass window at Roncesvalles United Church and in the first law in North America granting trans folk human rights. I miss her. I miss her humour, her friendship, and her music. I'm always thrilled when I get a chance to see the stained-glass window again. It remains a place that trans folk go to have their photo taken, a true place of pilgrimage.

Remember Bernice? I told of her in my prologue. I haven't run into Bernice in years, and I doubt she's still with us, but I would be doing her a gross disservice if I didn't reveal the glorious end to her story. Bernice, if you remember, was the older street-involved woman who said she couldn't join our table for dinner because she would drive the young men at that table "wild with lust." She did eventually join our table for dinner that night, seating herself next to those same young men. One of those young men apparently was, if not driven wild with lust, taken enough with Bernice to eventually ask her to marry him! I performed their wedding during an evening service, and it was one of the most joyful I've ever officiated. It cost them nothing. The wedding clothes came from Goodwill, the food from our local food bank. We were going to have dinner anyway. The evening service folk attended, but so did many of the morning folk. Bernice's young man was more than twenty years her junior. Neither she, he, nor anybody cared a twig.

How little do we understand the women in our lives? How badly do we understand the divine mysteries of sexuality, gender, motivations, the actions of the Holy Spirit in our lives? How poorly do we comprehend the powerful force of love? What do we know?

I marvel at us. To all the queers, socialists, street folk, women who've blown my mind over the years, you have, with the Divine as your helper, changed everything. You've cracked the world open so that the light can shine in.

This is a love letter to all of you.

Blessings.

EPILOGUE

JUST DO THE IMPOSSIBLE

s I finish writing this book, a global uprising against anti-Black racism is in effect. Unprecedented reforms to policing and "business as usual" are taking place. Like the Indigenous uprisings, rail blockades, refusal to cede territories to big oil and gas projects, these movements give us all hope for our earth. Sadly, though, unless they result in the kind of revolution that displaces our economic system and brings about a real democracy—that is, a system run for people and not profit—reforms are all we will ever get. However, like this tale of one woman's life, reforms are not nothing. Reforms are crucial. They change our lives as they are lived now—not in some utopian future. So we can hold two truths together: reform and revolution.

If there's one lesson I've learned, it's that reform and revolution aren't contradictory. I've also learned another, the twelve-step mantra of "progress not perfection." I personally call it "the joy of sin." We're all joyously fallible, traumatized, wanting humans. If we are loved by anyone and love anyone, our lives include holiness. That's the other theme.

I hope this book can be seen as something of a manual for how, in spite of our own "messiness," we can be change agents. I also hope it will inspire women, particularly racialized, trans, street-involved, and queer women, to engage in the political world. Yes, even mainstream bourgeois state politics.

The "Squad" in the U.S. Congress (Alexandria Ocasio-Cortez, Ilhan Omar, Ayanna Pressley, and Rashida Tlaib) shows the way. We should take heart knowing that even in the U.S., socialist racialized women can get elected. Closer to home, I think of Jody Wilson-Raybould, who wasn't a "team player," instead holding to principle. Far from a socialist, she is just a woman speaking truth to power. It cost her.

The most important lesson I learned is that once elected, it's critical to stay true to the principles you came with. Those principles are almost guaranteed to get you into trouble with your own party and the powerful forces that influence the political agenda. Relish those moments. Learn to see the importance of exactly those moments. That's the Divine's way of letting you know you're on the right path. If your highest calling is re-election or the Party, no matter which party it is, you may find yourself with more obvious power, but way, way less purpose.

Listen to the activists. Be an activist and an advocate. If you do, you're almost certain to fail, of course. So what? As a Christian, I can say I follow one of the world's great failures, Jesus. He (They) had a short career, three years or so, whittled His (Their) followers down to a handful of women, and then died an excruciating death. Doesn't get worse.

In contrast, the women I've loved and learned from and I have been amazingly lucky. A few slings and arrows of outrageous fortune, but I'm intact, in a job I love, with loving children. I'm honoured and grateful for all the places I've been allowed to be, including one of those green leather seats at Queen's Park. I don't harbour any illusions about myself, but along with most women I know, we think less of ourselves, sadly, than anyone else could. We are often our own most unfair critics. So perhaps our real hurdle is actually understanding that even though 90 percent of the portraits on the walls of power are of men, and men are (aren't they?) the great philosophers, theologians, theorists, and so on, the only difference between us and them is power. They have it and we still, by comparison, don't.

There's so much left to do. We are in the midst of an environmental crisis that will end life on earth as we know it, but our governments aren't doing much of anything. We also know if what we do in response to this existential crisis is done without justice, without working with those who are excluded, it will be worthless. If economic viability means the status quo, it isn't viable. Capitalism, meaning continual growth, is the true utopian fantasy. We're living its reality with continuous war and earth's destruction. The role of religion as giving us tools so as to be "happy" in our current state is the true heresy. Faith demands action, an action out of love.

This requires those who are in faith communities to act as well. To reform their own faith homes. That's as uneasy as telling the truth about our own lives. Telling the truth about your life is one of the most difficult actions, particularly within faith communities. So, yes, telling the truth in church as in the state takes some courage. Sir Walter Raleigh, author of "The Lie," quoted throughout this book, was executed for his truth-telling. The good news in this country is that it's unlikely you'll be beheaded for your truth. So risk it. Risk being your own street-involved, queer, socialist, faithful you.

For the faithful, no matter what faith, your scriptures need to be held up, not ignored. It's the right-wing, exclusive, racist, homo-/bi-/transphobic versions of our faiths that aren't scripturally faithful. Get rid of the theological bathwater, not the baby!

"Now we see in a glass darkly, then we will see face to face," says Paul in 1 Corinthians 13:12. At the end of the day, we're as important and as insignificant as it gets. Truly, though, we are also created in the image of the Divine and the Divine is messy. From the 1970s with our fringe and utopian asks for the queer community, to this moment when the climate crisis calls us to change the way we function in almost every way, we have to be realistic, now more than ever.

Demand the impossible. Do the impossible.

APPENDIX

A STATEMENT

from the Honourable Tracy MacCharles regarding the Reverend Doctor Cheri DiNovo

The courage of the first mover is rarely recognized at the time of the action. The vision that progressive thinkers possess, while often radical in their day, are the things of which we are proud only a short time later.

I am sorry that Reverend DiNovo had to go through the ordeal that she did and that anyone had to go through those difficulties at what should have been one of the happiest moments of their lives.

It is a sadness that it takes retrospection, and the passage of time, to give due credit to the bravery of the people who helped us to remember that love is love and it comes with no qualifiers.

The actions of the previous Ontario Conservative government under Mike Harris and Bob Runciman are regrettable and unfortunate.

I encourage the current leadership of the Ontario Conservative Party to take ownership of this dark moment in the history of a once great political party.

I'm extremely proud of the work of our Government, and that of our Premier as an ally and advocate for the LGBTQ2S community in promoting acceptance, respect and diversity.

We were the first jurisdiction in North America to recognize same-sex marriage and the third jurisdiction in the world to do so.

As a province, we agreed that the time had come to modernize our Physical Education Curriculum to include a spectrum of sexual orientations and identities. We changed designations on birth certificates and other legal documents to "parent" to be more inclusive of same-sex and nonbinary families.

We also introduced legislation that ensured that parents who use egg or sperm donors or surrogates do not have to adopt their own children.

The Conservatives, under this present leader, have expressed a desire to take us back. He would have us go back to a day where this anachronistic thinking would be considered normal.

I am proud of how strong of an ally our Government and Premier have been to the LGBTQ2S community and of marriage equality.

It is my sincere desire that no person should ever have to endure the hardships faced by Cheri DiNovo and others in the course of doing what is right and what is just.

Tracy MacCharles, MPP Pickering-Scarborough East
Minister of Government and Consumer Services
Minister Responsible for Accessibility

Grateful acknowledgement is made for permission to use an excerpt from "Prodigal Son" by Robert Wilkins. © Wynwood Music Co., Inc. All rights reserved. Used with permission of Wynwood Music Co., Inc.